Five Steps
Distracted Churches
Who Leave Their *First* Love

"To the angel of the church in Ephesus write:
But I have this against you, that you have abandoned the love
you had at first." Revelation 2:4

Finding the Missional Path

Barry E. Winders

Finding the Missional Path
by Barry E. Winders

Printed in the United States of America

ISBN 978-1-60266-817-1

www.xulonpress.com

Table of Contents

Acknowledgements

This book would not exist without the love, support, and belief of my wife, Carmen. Since the day we met she has encouraged me to follow my passion. Carmen, thank you for believing in me during this project.

Thanks goes to Reggie McNeal, author of *The Present Future,* for encouraging the development of more missional talk. When I met Reggie in November 2005, in Jefferson City, Missouri, he affirmed what I believed already in my heart. He spoke of the church as a "club" and pointed out to those of us who were there how the church in North America as we know it, is not reaching people.

Also thanks to everyone who volunteered to be part of this three-year project and for your understanding of what it takes to create change in others. There have been many hours devoted to speaking, writing, and rewriting. But it has been worth it.

Also thanks to Rev. Luther Rhodes and his friendship, Dr. Vyron Yount for his laughter and support.

Special thanks go to Rev. John H. Rice and Rev. Sam Roethemeyer. For all the support and fun you gave me at Bent Creek golf course.

Thanks to my sales associates at Staples Super Office Store in Cape Girardeau, Missouri, Paul Miranda, Don Edwards, John Brown, Brenda Murphy, Lynn Corn, Christopher Smiddy, Dustin Hill, Joe Bisagno, David Pepon, Stephen Peel, Kyle Rees and the rest of the people at Staples for their belief in me.

Most of all, I thank my God that He always knew what He wanted to do with me. Sometimes I felt alone but I know I was never alone. God has lifted me when I needed a spiritual lift and snatched me away from the hurtful remarks of the pious.

Introduction

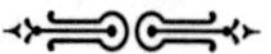

In 1999, I resigned a pastorate in Illinois after 12 years driven by the compulsion to grow a church. Indeed, the congregation had grown during the time from a congregation of 130 to over 600 in attendance. Fortunately for me, I was a young man in my late 30's and was able to keep up with the demanding pace of assimilating members, recruiting and training volunteers, coaching leaders, monitoring programs and progress. Church growth consumed my attention. I attended almost every church growth conference within 300 miles. Multiple hours were spent reading all the books and magazine articles I could find on the subject of church growth. I had become adept in analyzing demographics, understanding subsets of people groups, compiling statistics, charts and graphs. I learned how to obtain and interpret measurable results and tweak whatever needed tweaking. You name it. I had become a consumer and proprietor of church growth ideas to every pastor and church leader within my circle of influence. Of course, notoriety, not for my own good was the subsequent result. Soon I became a target of other envious pastors and most of all Satan drew a huge bulls-eye on my back.

At the end of the day, my family and I had paid a tremendous price for the long hours devoted to growing a church or at the very minimum, thinking about it. However, I committed a huge mistake. I had neglected my wife, our relationship and especially my relationship with my daughter. At the impressionable age of 17, she rebelled and ran away from home. It marked the end of a successful twelve year run of growing a church but not without a heavy price. I paid dearly. The shocking reality was that I was unsuccessful as a father and husband and it was both obvious and public.

Worse yet, the church was not part of any of the restoration process that was to follow. The local church in Illinois and even other churches and leaders within this small, rural, Baptist group that knew me well as a preacher's kid and also as a minister, did not offer any help for our situation. Tragically, all of them were too consumed with their own church stuff and their own compulsion of growing and attracting people to their church to comfort any casualties like us on the open road.

My critics told me the problem was burnout and sin in my life and that I should accept being a casualty of the church and that it was of my own doings. They offered no solutions to me only condemnation. Most of my friends were like the friends Job had in the Bible. They walked around me, starred at my plight, saw my need yet quietly stood by. Soon, they then moved on. Yes, that's right. They moved on with their lives. My relational graveyard was apparent. My entire family received little tangible support although I am sure prayers were offered up for our situation. Fortunately, in one way my family no longer existed out there on the conversation circuit. In another way, I felt no one continued to say our names before God in prayer.

However, there was one exception. One compassionate church pastor in Jackson, Missouri, where I served alongside him as a staff member, showed enormous support and total trust in me. This pastor, and of course, God, brought us through. The first six years after the initial tragedy occurred I consistently allowed God to make repairs in my life by forgiving me of my relationship failures via spiritual formation. Thanks to God, He had done the unthinkable and the unimaginable. During this time, He returned our daughter back to us. We were healed relationally and so was she. What a mighty God we serve!

Looking back on the past, I saw several church leaders leaning over people's shoulders giving rapid condemning remarks. In the distance, I saw training under way in glass houses of worship throwing stones and totally unaware they were distracted from being the church God had called precisely called them to be. Then, one day a defining moment occurred. During a conversation with a non-churchgoer framed a huge question. "Have you thought about changing the way church leaders love humanity?" He asked. "How can we change the way churches love humanity, when we can't change anyone else's behavior? I replied. Then the answer came. "Well," I said, "it sounds like we need a whole new approach."

This book outlines that new approach to distracted churches who leave their first love as mentioned in the Bible. It is for busy pastors, leaders, and followers who want to improve their loving quotient, and are ready to transform missionally their congregations by trying something new. It is for the pastor who would like to be more effective at inspiring missional transformation among churchgoers in the workplace, home, school, and neighborhood. It is for the ministry leadership team who are ready to take on changing the culture of a whole organization

This new approach is what I call "Finding the Missional Path." Missional path leaders are courageous at bringing out the main thing with the church. They refocus the church's vision—_literally reframing our conversations about church.

Finding the Missional Path is a practical, five-step guide to a new way of viewing church, based on the missionary purpose of God.

The Five Steps

Here, in a brief overview, are the five steps that make up this missional transformation.

Step 1. Missional Spirituality—The Soul's Transformation

You will succeed in transforming the distraction of the church only if you believe capitalizing on the vision of God for loving humanity as Christ did. Some individuals have. Most churches in North American have not. Ask people point-blank "Is doing church or more of it the best way to reach people?" and, in most conversations people say they just want to see the church ***be*** the church.

If you count yourself in the overwhelming majority, you are going to have a hard time negotiating through the remaining steps.

So, in the first step, you'll examine your mind-set of the sentness of Christ, strangely empowered by it, and wanting to love what he loved, having our hearts broken for the same reason his was and rejoice in what brings him joy. This is missional spirituality.

Step 2. Missional Calling—The Soul's Passion

Armed with a first-love mindset, you will take the next step: nourishing and developing your soul to be ready for transformational change. There is a principle here for spiritual leaders who want to see their organization move beyond their distraction. To just talk about what is needed, to hold conferences, or even to post some new set of values or mission statements on the whiteboard is not enough.

Research shows it will take an organization ten to fifteen years to embrace those values even with a consistent and satisfactory job by the leaders in verbal communication.

However, if we as leaders nourish the missional calling and attach actions to the way our souls are being formed, and make it part of our leadership behavior, it may only require about three years to bring about the culture change desired for the church. **We** must act the way we want our transformed churches to be—even if it feels like we are pretending at first. We cannot wait until we feel like it. We must act our way into a feeling than to feel our way into an action.

Step 3. Missional Visioning—The Soul's Destination

In step three, you will learn the importance of the leader's ability to press forward through uncertainty. You will encounter the author's concept of The Dwelling Principle based on Psalm 23. You will learn how this principle helps us to express the benefits of recognizing God's presence in The Kitchen of the Soul, The Basement of the Heart, and the Living Room of Human and Divine Presence.

You will become handy with two tools: one that helps you to generate ideas about how your spiritual journey takes you through twists and turns, and another that puts these ideas into practice. Understanding the movements of our faith help us to face, recognize, and articulate the raw human emotion before God. In other words, it will bring about a naked honesty with ourselves before the Almighty.

Step 4. Missional Learning—The Soul's Searching

You will get off the missional path quickly if you do not know how to navigate away from those activities that return you to old ways of thinking. For several reasons, this proves challenging. First, because it takes a lot of discipline and creativity to stop doing what distracts you from seeing with God's missional eyes.

Second, because, even if you generate some new ideas, it is hard to not feel guilty, feel isolated and in the minority when you start to put these ideas into practice.

Third, because, as people talk about it, most of us do not think we should criticize the church and we should steer away from what is predictable and what has always been known as church.

So, bring all of your resolve to step four. What you will learn here is how that your mission and mine are not inside the walls of the church. Why can't the school including students, faculty, and parents, be the mission for a teacher? Why can't the spiritual immaturity of a husband be the mission for a wife?

Step 5. Missional Accountability—The Soul's Seriousness

In this step, you will notice that something has radically changed. What if everybody saw themselves as a missionary and not a minister as we were formally conditioned and trained to believe? You will begin to see how important it is to notice how many people in your church are released to be missional instead of how many are involved in worthwhile church job to sustain the institution.

I believe the Five Steps are useful at every organizational level: from enabling pastors to better develop their people, to transforming distracted churches and distracted denominations, judicatories, and state initiatives.

The central part of this book, the missional diagrams, points to a new way of thinking, a new way of listening, and a new approach to every conversation a leader has with their people.

I have tried to make the book as readable as possible, simplifying complex ideas by using metaphor and analogy, and creating illustrations where I can. If the book gets to be heavy going at any point, try jumping to the missional diagrams to see how they are being used in context. You may find this a handy reference.

In Revelation 2:4, Jesus reminded the church at Ephesus they had abandoned their first love. They had excelled in good works toward others by showing patience and forbearance. They were proficient in preserving church discipline by exposing sin, false teachers, and those who were deceivers of the truth.

For the Ephesian Church, abandoning the *first* love did not mean she had forsaken the object of it, but instead her members had lost the fervent degree of that *first* love by growing remiss and cold toward God and others. Paul spent three years in Ephesus and knew the church and community well.

Later, he presented to leaders a bold account recorded in Acts 20:36-38 RSV when the Ephesian Christians were most affectionate and loving to him, to God, and to others. This was his description of the *first* love.

Paul's missional campaign in Ephesus and Asia Minor was a result of his decision to expand his work from the synagogue, where it was confined and denied necessary freedom.

"To the angel of the church in Ephesus write: The words of him who holds the seven stars in his right hand, who walks among the seven golden lampstands. I know your works, your toil and your patient endurance, and how you cannot bear evil men but have tested those who call themselves apostles but are not, and found them to be false; I know you are enduring patiently and bearing up for my name's sake, and you have not grown weary. But I have this against you, that you have abandoned the love you had at first." Revelation 2:4 RSV

Traditionally, preachers have used this verse to motivate believers to remember the conversion event or salvation experience. They are only partially correct. What Jesus likely had in mind was the essence, not the event, in every Christian's *first* love to participate in God's worldwide redemptive mission, which is experienced around the early days of conversion and salvation.

When I consider my *first* love, upon my profession of faith at age 8, I was strongly encouraged to do next the most awesome thing. Minutes after I prayed, confessed my sins, and received Christ into my heart, a young country preacher (who just happened to be my father) in a small rural Baptist Church insisted that I go tell somebody. My first love included both total acceptance and a missional challenge to evangelize because of the missional sentness of both scripture and experience. In other words, an infinite God accepted my humanity and placed upon it the highest possible value in all creation, becoming the conduit through which the Savior communicates His love. Isn't that remarkable?

The Premise of the Book

Let us consider for a moment, what would be the focus of church culture if she abandoned her *first* love as spoken about in The Book of Revelation? By no means am I suggesting that every church in America has lost their *first* love. However, when that occurs, the church must understand two things.

Without missional transformation, a "good" but certainly not "great" effort characterizes church ministry and church behavior. Abandoning our *first* love sharply reduces the effectiveness of church members to carry God's message in their lifestyle and proclamation. When church members immerse themselves deeply in church stuff (equating what we do with what God wants done), this abandonment can occur.

When distractions move to the front burner, "*first* love" is abandoned. Church stuff, controversial subjects, cultural viewpoints, politics, and a plethora of side issues become "first" in our church life.

So, how do distractions become the primary focus? The Bible defines our first love and shapes our assumptions far less than we like to admit. Often, American Christians are concerned with "abortion," "gay marriage," and "stem cell research," more that the comprehensive mission of God in America.

Unfortunately, the missional concern of our missionary God remains unexamined. The church bogs down with more and more church stuff by preserving the institution, using borrowed tools of modernity to do church, and in some cases outsourcing their evangelistic opportunities to peripheral issues.

So, what do these distractions look like and how will the church redirect its interest? What areas of interest or obsession could possibly place the church in a defensive mode that leads to misdirected attention? Further, how serious are the implications of neglecting the *first* love upon church members? What can church leadership do to help church members rediscover their *first* love?

At the end of the day, is the North American church culture turning Christianity into a temple-based religion? Is the church too busy managing the institution to manage its future? Will the church stop flirting with the idolatrous self-delusion of having prominence in society to starting discussions about how the church is going to impact a pluralistic society where Christianity's religious turf is being challenged by other religions? Is the church today too obsessed with political activism, numbers and techniques while missing the culture's real hunger to experience the Spirit?

Of greater concern is the American culture's hunger for the holy, the mysterious, the unexplainable, and the spiritual? People today are pressing all the spiritual "hot" buttons searching for purpose and for understanding of their role in God's redemptive mission in the world. At times it appears church members are sending the wrong message to their membership by urging them to save the institution. Paradoxically, whatever we spend our efforts to save, we end up losing. Not released to be missional in their homes, schools, neighborhoods and places of work, church members sense a conflict of mission because the Great Commandment and the Great Commission stated in the Bible differs from the primary focus of the church. What a dilemma! The aim of the church must be souls—not just saved souls but formed souls.

The Purpose of the Book

At the core of this book is an attempt to answer three questions:

1. Is North American church culture turning Christianity into a temple-based religion?

2. In what ways are many churches distracted from the mission of God, outsourcing evangelism opportunities and missing the culture's hunger to experience the Spirit?

3. How can church leaders be missional and utilize the five steps to transform distracted churches who abandon their first love?

The purpose of this book is to challenge church leaders to release their church members from institutional "propping up" so they will return to their abandoned *first* love and accept the missional challenge to develop a missionary sensitivity to engage post-Christian culture where interest in spirituality is increasing and participation in institutional religion is waning.

Finding the Missional Path is a book written to help churches turn their members into missionaries; fully empowered by the Spirit of God and who see themselves as being sent to experience God's mission to Western Culture. Accepting the challenge of releasing members from meaningless "church stuff" is daunting. Church professionals and leaders may resist it due to their modern seminary training or of years of practice. Clergy, priests, bishops, and leaders know best how to perpetuate the burden of institutionalism by handcuffing their constituents to the religious institution thus making it run like a machine.

While denominational structures continue, their distinctions begin to blur and fade as the issue of kingdom living takes center stage. Indeed, the various denominations recognize how people have begun to view followers of Jesus less and less as a church group or new ministry idea. Instead, they view themselves as genuinely good at moving away from a confining, non-liberating religion in order to follow hard after Jesus. The self-identity of these Jesus followers is in churches and they are outside of the churches.

The author's intent is not to make blatant charges against the church without supporting evidence. I have no "axe to grind" or unwarranted criticism for the church. In fact, I enthusiastically continue to serve the local church hopeful to be part of a clergy-led, leader-led movement to see the church think big and pursue a bold vision to prioritize evangelism by engaging in activities that release church members to complete the emphasis of the Great Commission of making disciples.

In *Finding the Missional Path*, the author unpacks the church's self-deception about institutional religion. These acts of delusion, by claiming a one-dimensional view of things, turn a blind eye to all other ways of seeing things, including God's way. This book contends that the church has confined its missional beliefs by equipping its members to do ministry activity only inside its four walls. In other words, the church is holding itself captive from the tumultuous world outside. In the words of Os Guinness, "There is always tension in unbelief because the truth remains the truth even when we hold truth hostage." [1]

The greatest challenge facing churches today is to live missionally: to develop missionary sensitivity to postmodern culture, vision, and practices, and to engage in God's mission with the post-Christian culture around it. By not addressing this fundamental challenge, all the efforts to reform the institution so it may "keep up" or "survive" cultural insurgency are futile.

Today, this missional challenge is central to and carried by our *first* love, and represents a profound learning curve for most churches and a remarkable opportunity for church leaders. As Christians, there are times in our journey when all of us fail to detect losing the first love. It frequently happens due to the serious times we live in. It happens to all of us when we are busy doing "church stuff." It is so easy to lose sight of the power, the challenge, and the missional transformation predicated by *first* love.

Churches who take seriously this missional posture will discern fully God's mission, understand the current cultural context, and discover how God has prepared "fields ripened unto harvest." As a result, church members, as well as church leaders, will learn together what it means to be the church in this highly interactive, participatory culture. Yet many churches are not missional because their members are not missional. Members who rediscover their first love experience missional transformation because they have aligned themselves with the heart and passion of Jesus!

Trapeze artists fully understand this wisdom and its consequences. When one concentrates too intently on getting safely across the chasm, the risk of falling increases. Moreover, the risks increase exponentially for the performer who concentrates on *not* falling.

Confident high-wire artists train themselves to be relevant and in the present, feeling sublimely confident so that reaching the other side is a forgone conclusion. Nothing is more important than exhibiting poise during the crossing. The church should do the same. After all, God promised *"Every valley shall be raised up, every mountain and hill made low; the rough ground shall become level, the rugged places a plain. And the glory of the Lord will be revealed, and all mankind together will see it. For the mouth of the Lord has spoken"* (Isaiah 40:4-5 NIV).

Again, *first* love definitely leads to missional transformation because it reframes our conversations about being the church. Missional transformation happens when we begin thinking like a missionary here in the U.S. Further, missional transformation provides the "great escape" from church stuff, disembedding Christianity from its modern trappings and re-embedding it in the new emerging world.

Throughout the book, we will examine the discipline of turning away from our distractions and finding our way back onto the missional path. We will see how critical it is to succeed in turning this vague conviction that something must change into a daily discipline that leads us toward the thing we all covet: a church where we can declare our mission as being our job, our home, our school or our neighborhood: a mission where we can flourish.

To start the journey, you must at least consider the possibility that what is stopping you and your church from being the church is not programs and resources. These are all external circumstances that may play some role but certainly not a major one.

You must consider the possibility that what is stopping you is what you believe; that in effect you are stopping yourself. Over the years, you have come to believe some things, and these beliefs (some of them are distractions) are now so deeply entrenched that no matter what new discipline you learn, and no matter how favorable your circumstances become, you will never be the church. You must return to your first love. Your problem is not that you do not know how to or that no one will let you. It is that you are not even trying. Until now.

Chapter One

ABANDONING OUR FIRST LOVE–DISTRACTED BY CHURCH STUFF

To accept the truth about what I am, as also the truth about other human beings, demands courage.

–Michael Casey [1]

Introduction

Somewhere in his writings, Danish philosopher *Soren Kierkegaard* tells a story about a circus that came to his native town in Denmark. The circus troupe's agenda was to come into a community, handout flyers announcing the performances, and to set up a big tent on the on the outskirts of town. One day the big top tent caught on fire an hour before the evening show. Ironically, the only performer dressed was one of the clowns who ran into the nearby village crying for help. When the townspeople saw the clown, they were amused by his hand waving, and loud, verbal outbursts. They perceived he was only up to his usual clown antics. They did not comprehend he was frantically shouting for their help! It was not until they looked past the clown, saw the red glow on the horizon, that they realized there was an emergency. According to Kierkegaard, "they heard the clown with their eyes." The crowd assumed the clown was on a mission to drum up business.[2]

I enjoy telling Kierkegaard's story because it serves as a reminder of how we all make assumptions, clouded by the clutter of preconceived expectations (stuff) which often serve as the purpose for what we believe is real. In a similar way, church stuff occupies our minds and causes us to believe that serving the church and its busyness (sometimes disguised as ministry) diverts our attention from our first love and mission. When this occurs, evangelism of unreached people becomes something we Christians notice, but do not have time to do. Soon, church stuff has diverted our spiritual focus. Little wonder that many Christians say all they want to do is worship God and view their mission as their home, their school, and their workplace because they are more comfortable in starting and joining spiritual conversations in those environments.

Conversely, as church leaders we eagerly instruct new believers to identify their spiritual gifts via some spiritual gifts inventory in order to quickly assimilate them into the church. The problem with this strategy is two-fold. One, every church leader knows of laity jobs with vacancies that need to be filled, and we have all been coached by church growth proponents that these filled vacancies become so called "holding tanks" for the new believers to stay connected and involved. Soon, if we are not careful, the new believer can get the idea that the church wants them to be busy with church stuff, while the spiritual formation of their soul starves to death.

Second, as leaders, we overlook that many of these new believers want to learn more about Jesus and how the Christian life can aid their current life situations. In other words, new believers want some life coaching concerning their future before they sign up for church positions. Imagine that! Since 9/11, the world has changed significantly and no place has changed more in its spiritual questing for God than in America. It is clear that religion in America is in a state of transition. Will religion take on the influences of the East emerging as an entirely new religion that offers a sustainable worship and a less privatized faith? Will religion be woven into the fabric of everyday living with many church attenders viewing their workplace, their homes, their neighborhoods, and their schools as their mission? I believe so. George Mair, author of *A Life With Purpose* states, "In the aftermath of the tragedy, people have become more curious about other faiths. The need to understand the roots of the world's conflicts has led to an increased desire to learn about religion. But the larger effect of the 9/11 tragedy has been the new quest for comfort from the fear generated by the attacks. The sudden realization that the world changed forever on that tragic day gave many men and women cause to reconsider. Suddenly, life was bigger, more important, and in dire need of explanation. Many looked for those answers in church." [3]

I believe spiritual life on this side of 9/11 can be interpreted remarkably different than it was before. American culture is noticeably unsatisfied with the answers the modern era has given concerning life and purpose. Now that the culture seems to be hungering for spiritual answers to their questions, ironically the church is not equipped and certainly not focused on providing those answers. In other words, millions of unchurched people are spiritually active. In Barna's 2005 research, he contends,

> "During a typical month, six out of ten unchurched adults worship God (but not via church services); three out of ten study the Bible; and one out of every seven have times of prayer and Bible reading with family members."
>
> "The more important trend, however, is that a large and growing number of Americans who avoid congregational contact are not rejecting Christianity as much as they are shifting how they interact with God and people in a strategic effort to have a more fulfilling spiritual life." [4]

In the future, will today's teenagers, evolve back to pre-church-growth movement ideals and desire a more apostolic-led missionary church in quest for a genuine expression of spirituality and missional transformation?

I believe we are on the precipice of a new era of spiritual experience and expression. This emerging generation identified by Barna as the Mosaics were born from 1984-2002. Barna suggests, "These mosaics are not like any previous generation—they have a new eclectic, nonlinear way of thinking." [5]

These Mosaics see that many parents have messed up their own lives and do not have the background to address the spiritual concerns of children and teenagers. Much of today's church leadership is comprised of Baby Boomers who are enthralled with being a successful church. So much of the time, they talk about programs, buildings, number of members, not how their lives have been changed by a relationship with Christ. Let's be honest here. Didn't Jesus die on the cross to change lives and not to build bigger buildings with more people? As you read this section, do you hear your church members crying for release from mundane busy work at the church and instead be re-trained and equipped as missionaries to their homes, schools, places of work and neighborhoods? Would you like to be an instrument in God's hand? Like Moses, could you lead the church to an exodus (escape) far away from modern church growth, which uses the ideology and borrowed tools of Egypt and helps the church to be comfortable in its own captivity?

Dan Kimball, a forty-two-year-old pastor of the Vintage Faith Church in Santa Cruz, California, is the author of *The Emerging Church*. Kimball believes that these young Mosaic Christians (tomorrow's leaders) are not pleased with the current church shopping list of opportunities and rituals. Kimball says, "These dissatisfied young worshippers find that the mega-churches feel like Wal-Mart, that the pastors sound like Tony Robbins with some Bible verses, and the music is like a pep rally. They want to know 'Where are the crosses? Where's the expression of spirituality?'"[6] Doesn't that rattle your cage a little bit? Doesn't it make you want to breakout of modern church professionalism and "slick" advertising to just "be" the church?

And what about spiritual formation? Interestingly, young people are returning to the church with renewed interest in church history, in the spiritual practices and readings of church fathers such as Wesley, Luther, Calvin, St. John of the Cross, St. Catherine of Genoa, C.S. Lewis, Dallas Willard, Richard Foster, Todd Hunter, Larry Crabb and others. Interest in house churches and adult spiritual formation groups are on the rise. These young crusaders of the church want more than a Sunday school class where fellowship around donut rings and coffee is the goal of the day. Instead, they are spiritual questing for a spirituality that is useful in their everyday lives. Pause now for a moment. Has the modern church strayed from all this? I am ashamed to admit it but we have.

So, will these new mosaic Christians return to white steeple churches? Less multimedia? More story telling? More classical hymns of the ancient church? Perhaps more traditional music? I do not know. One thing is for sure. This new emerging generation is on a journey for the real and the genuine. I believe they intend to learn how to live with less comfort because they have witnessed the "hole in the hearts" or spiritual vacuum of the previous generation. All this has led younger Christians to believe that perhaps modernity Christians have overlooked the profound in the simple, the extraordinary in the ordinary, and most of all, the Holy Spirit of our Triune God.

With some pretense in saying this, I honestly apologize for the lack of humility of my generation. Convenience and comfort have imprisoned us within the walls of the church. As churchgoers, we have wanted more for ourselves and have fed into this national desire for even more yet.

One of my favorite movies in recent years is *Shawshank Redemption*. It is about a young, entrepreneurial banker named Andy Dufresne played by Tim Robbins, sentenced to life in prison for killing his wife; a murder he did not commit. Several years went by. He made numerous friends on the inside namely 'Red' Redding by actor Morgan Freeman. He worked as the prison librarian and later, handled the financial affairs of the warden himself, discovering the warden's misappropriation of prison funds. His prison life adjustments could not dampen his restless spirit and personal dream to be free somewhere on a Caribbean beach with his own sailboat. One night his dream became reality when he successfully escaped prison authorities along with a lucrative amount he acquired in a double-crossed money scam with the warden who trusted him completely. By the time the warden learned of Andy's escape with all the "dough", it was too late. The frantic, outsmarted warden committed suicide just minutes before members of the governor's office and state officials knocked on his door to arrest him. The movie ends with a scene that showed middle-aged Andy on a sunny beach polishing his sailboat. Consider the many nights Andy must have lain awake in his cell rehearsing and planning his escape or his *first* love. When the time came for the breakout, he had more than enough courage to go through with it.

As church leaders, it would serve us well to envision our own breakout by returning to our early *first* love of Christ and our participation in his missionary purpose. If we cast a new vision, intentionally will a planned escape from saving the religious institution to saving lost humanity, we will not have to worry about finding the courage to do it. Let us prayerfully petition our gracious God.

God grant me the serenity
to accept the things I cannot change,
Courage to change the things I can,
and wisdom to know the difference.
Reinhold Neibur

I agree with Erwin MaManus who said, "Christianity has become our Shawshank, and our redemption will only come if we find the courage to escape the prison we have created for ourselves. Risking everything to live free is our only hope—humanity's only hope." [7]

What does first love mean for God and Jesus?

Many biblical passages could be examined to help us understand the Trinitarian relationship of God and Jesus. But the most important one is found in John 5:16-30. In every case, Jesus is the obedient one. The Son obeys the Father. It is a functional subordination where the Father sends, the Father commands, the Father shows, the Father commissions, and the Son obeys. It is never the other way.

Notice in verses 19 through 21. "For only what he sees the Father doing; for whatever he does, that the Son does likewise; for the Father loves the Son, and shows him all that he himself is doing; for as the Father raises the dead and gives them life, so also the Son gives life to whom he will."

In other words, whatever the Son does it is a reflection of what the Father does. Why? Because the Son loves the Father and he always does what the Father gives him to do. That is extraordinary language!

The theological and Christological implication to all of this is the Son, by his obedience, is acting in such a way that he is revealing the Father. And, if Jesus does what his Father does, he does so because he loves the Father. Then, when only he says what the Father gives him to say, and does only what the Father gives him to do, he is doing so because he loves the Father.

This *first* love and perfection of Jesus' disclosing of God himself to us is certainly bound up in his obedience. Do you find that striking? I do. This means that Jesus disclosed God to us in the first order or the first instance not because he loved us, but because he loves the Father. Now this is not saying Jesus does not love us. He does. But in order for Jesus to perfectly and completely love us, the intra-trinitarian *first* love in the very Godhead has to be there. The heart of Jesus' own missional spirituality was wrapped up first and foremost in his obedience. This was partly what drove Jesus to the Cross. In other words, Jesus wants to do everything the Father gives him to do and everything the Father gives him to say. He goes to the cross in the first place because he cries in the garden "Not my will but yours be done."

At the end of the day, Jesus said to his followers, "Have I been with you such a long time and you have not known me?" "He who has seen me, has seen the Father." This is truly remarkable. The marvelous self-disclosure of the Father and the Son, guarantees that God's love for us is mediated through his Son. This means that the special revelation of God through Christ turns not solely on God's love for us but God's love for his Son. Christ's redemptive work for us is based on his *first* love for his Father. This is why Jesus did those things that pleased God. This perfected love between Jesus and God is a first love born out of perfect obedience. Jesus can be to us what he was to the Father because together they modeled what it is to know first love. Bottom line. The purpose of God is that all may honor the Son just as they honor the Father according to John 5:23. That makes God a good father who wants the Son to reflect his love in perfect obedience by saying and doing precisely all that God says and does.

What does *first* love mean for us?

First love is God's total acceptance of humanity. Our *first* love is the understanding of the first encounter we initially have with God, which is a unilateral and unconditional relationship. Let me explain. The Bible teaches that while we were sinners, Christ demonstrated His unique love for us by dying for us and making atonement for our sins. This unique love, which in essence becomes our *first* love, is totally unilateral and initiated by God toward us. We can do nothing to provoke it, deserve it, earn it, or be good enough for it. Yet, we are the beneficiaries of God's love and grace. As the Scripture teaches, *"For by grace are you saved through faith; and not of yourselves. It is the gift of God, not of works, lest any man should boast" (Ephesians 2:8-9 KJV).*

This sense of grace becomes the foundation of all things, especially our lives and what we feel and what we do. To me, the act of conversion accomplishes much more than determining our eternal destiny. It accomplishes two things. One, conversion points out to us our value to God bestowed upon us from the beginning of our creation or human birth. It renames our primary existence as a gift not a need or accident. Two, conversion declares our flawed humanity of sinful warts and all transformed by total acceptance.

The classic Bible story about the woman caught in adultery recorded in John 8:1-11 best illustrates total acceptance by God. This encounter opens with the predicament of the woman. Caught in adultery, she has been shamed in the public eye and ridiculed. She is defenseless and branded openly a target for the righteous leaders of the synagogue.

The scribes and Pharisees are one up on her. They stand in a power position by making this woman appear before all. Then, these men tell Jesus that this woman was caught in adultery and the Law of Moses commands that she be stoned for her immorality. They ask Jesus about his position or judgment in the matter. The scribes and Pharisees hope to test Jesus by putting him on the spot while projecting their own self-righteousness.

Notice what Jesus does next. He bent down and wrote with his finger something we do not know on the ground. Then he makes the statement. *"Let him who is without sin among you be the first to throw a stone at her" (John 8:7 RSV)*. Then Jesus wrote on the ground a second time. Within seconds, this woman's accusers left Jesus alone with the woman.

Interestingly, this woman was about to experience *first* love and more importantly, total acceptance. *"Jesus looked up and said to her, Woman, where are they? Has no one condemned you? She said, No one, Lord. And Jesus said, Neither do I condemn you; go, and do not sin again" (John 8:10-11 RSV).*

Like this woman, haven't we all experienced what it is like to be caught? Maybe you were caught in a lie, making gossip about someone's reputation, or simply taking credit for something you did not do. Nevertheless, all of us have had our hands "slapped" for breaking a rule or law. What we remember most is the grace we received or failed to receive. We all desire to be completely forgiven, completely exonerated and completely released so we can move forward with our lives and find our mission for life. But our greatest need is total acceptance; more than forgiveness as we desire to be genuinely loved by God. This becomes our *first* love. Forgiveness without genuine love is like promising a child a gift only if they behave correctly and earn their parent's approval. Fortunately, this is not the kind of love offered by God. We do not have to become perfect, even according to his standards, in order to experience his love. God's *first* love is a free gift and we only needs to receive it. *"We love, because He first loved us" (1 John 4:19 RSV).*

Child psychologists tell us that a baby experiences acceptance and love in those early days after birth when the mother makes close-up eye contact with the infant. As the infant's vision improves and the frequency of their mother's face to face encounters increase, the infant's recognizes total acceptance and realizes security. As adults, we are no different. Face to face encounters with the Almighty's grace reveal the power to reshape and reform those areas of our lives in need of help. As flawed, imperfect humans, God loves us. This love is a law with God. It is a law he will never break. In other words, he can do no less than shine his accepting love on us. *Romans*

5:8 says, "But God shows his love for us in that while we were yet sinners Christ died for us." Knowing this can move us toward an acceptance of our own humanness and frailty.

An honest assessment of our standing in relation to God and to other people precedes transformation. This assessment helps us to not only approach God but to acknowledge the truth about ourselves, trusting in God's grace. Through God's graciousness comes a power to reshape and reform the areas of our life that need the most help. In other words, acceptance of our own frailty motivates us to pursue Christ's interceding grace in our lives.

Accepting our own frailty prepares us spiritually toward other people. Seeing ourselves as part of humanity and not separate helps us to admit that in our own weakness we rarely live up to God's image and are still in need of more of his grace. Therein lies acceptance. This new acceptance minimizes the potential for feelings of self-satisfaction or pride, which is the justification of ourselves that we are not like others. This was precisely the attitude of the Scribes and Pharisees toward the adulteress woman in scripture. This leads one to ask, how does our public accusations of another benefit us?

First Love is My Acceptance as Part of Humanity.

Secondly, our *first* love is the understanding of a continuing encounter with God's Kingdom rule over the world is a fiduciary relationship. There is much in this temporal life of ours that we are utterly powerless to change. As a child, I heard: "If you're ever going to amount to anything, you have to make something of yourself." I am sure those who said this meant it to be a dynamic motivation to make the most of what I had. But sometimes as children, these words of encouragement lead us to make incorrect conclusions. As someone once said, "Children are often excellent observers but poor interpreters." Children do not miss very much at all. When it comes to digesting humanity, they often miss the goal of solving every problem and answering every question. Truth is, even adults learn to place trust and confidence in God's control.

It is not my mission in life to right every wrong or find justice for every injustice. Nor is it my mission in life to think that I can straighten out the confused lives of everyone on this planet.

In my earlier ministry days, I grew fond of a song entitled *"Sheltered Safe Within the Arms of God."* This song gave hope to many of us who faced situations beyond our control and power to change. Those situations could only be given to God in prayer. Below are some of the words.

So let the storms rage high,
The dark clouds rise,
They don't worry me
For I'm sheltered safe within the arms of God
He walks with me
And naught of earth can harm me
For I'm sheltered safe within the arms of God.

Accepting our own humanity can open us to see through new lens with a new spirit toward others. Take the story, for example, about the adulteress woman mentioned earlier. In the narrative, this woman was forced to stand by herself before everyone. The actions of the scribes and Pharisees brought shame to her. Why do you think they made a public example of her? How did it benefit them? Let's go further. How do our public accusations of other people benefit us?

Do we bring public shame to others because we see ourselves separate from them and even generate a feeling of justification or pride that we are not like them? By doing so, we may feel justified and swell with an air of importance or superiority. But one thing is for sure. We can find deep acceptance when we see ourselves as part of frail humanity aware that we are unable to live up to the image of the divine in every situation. We will not always make godly choices. Once we accept our own frailty, we find ourselves, alongside others, receiving the gift of grace actualized in us. All of us, in our weakness, are unable to live up to the divine image God has placed upon us.

In this biblical narrative, the possibility of this woman's accusers to desire to pick up stones also raises the possible justification for the stones to be picked up against them. Are there other options rather than judgment and public shame? Clearly yes. Jesus chose the option of acceptance that opened up the possibility of transformation for the woman herself and her accusers.

Of course, the main argument that keeps people from accepting others is that they might not change and our acceptance could be misinterpreted to mean agreement. In his provocative book *No Perfect People Allowed*, author John Burke offers a counter argument to the larger argument. "If we accept others, are we accepting wrong behavior and therefore condoning things God clearly says are against his will—sinful? And if you have been fighting these thoughts, you are not the first. In Romans 6 Paul heads this fear off at the pass by saying, "*So since God's grace has set us free from the law, does this mean we can go on sinning? Of course not!*" But what he proceeds to show is that grace-based relationship is the only hope for authentic growth—there's no other option."[8]

Can we welcome people into our church who have obviously sinned and been caught in the act publicly without coming to terms with our own weaknesses in our lives? Pointing out the sins and evil doings of others can cause us to overlook the panorama of our own sin, which despite self-examination and self-disclosure lies hidden inside our cloaks of respectability.

The narrative in *John 8:11 RSV* leaves us with Jesus' concluding words: *"Neither do I condemn you; go, and do not sin again."* The Bible does not tell us if the woman ever sinned the same act again or if the accusers changed their attitude toward sinners. We simply do not know.

First Love Includes My Missional Challenge For the Sake of Humanity.

Our mission is to reconnect humanity to God. I believe we serve God best when we act humanely toward others and ourselves. In scripture and sacrament, in solitude and community, in engaging with neighbor and stranger—we experience God's disclosure of himself to us. His *first* love among us leads us to recognize our own community in humanity.

Erwin McManus in *The Barbarian Way* describes a raw and untamed faith waiting to be unleashed what seems strikingly similar to the *first* love Jesus desired for the church. He writes:

"The barbarian way is about love, intimacy, passion, and sacrifice. Barbarians love to live and live to love. For them God is life, and their mission is to reconnect humanity to Him. Their passion is that each of us might live in intimate communion with Him who died for us." [9]

Consider how the Samaritan woman at the well in *John 4:5-29* gained ownership of God's love, which transformed her shame that she felt in her initial experience with Christ. She becomes a witness of Jesus because of his self-disclosure. At story's end, she goes back to her community where people know her and speaks openly about Jesus by saying, *"Come, see a man who told me all that I ever did. Can this be the Christ?" (John 4:29 RSV)* Just think of it. This woman leaves Jesus to launch her own mission of telling others undisturbed by the fact that Jesus knew all about her past.

Ostensibly, the saga illustrates how our *first* love is a full disclosure of God himself, which leads us to a deeper knowledge of who we are which becomes missional indeed.

Prior to the woman's encounter with Jesus, she withheld herself from other villagers and risked revealing herself for fear of persecution and vulnerability. This becomes her pattern for living. It seemed hardly possible that later she would return to witness to the same villagers who knew the details of her past so well.

What enabled her to bravely acknowledge her own need and invite others to seek the same redemptive humanity she had found? How do such patterns of fear and hiding get broken?

When we reach across barriers as Jesus did, we clear a path to the place of failure that in turn becomes the place of recovery. It seems odd to say but this place of failure or reputation, (now cleansed by Jesus) becomes the most comfortable spot from which we attempt to join God's redemptive purpose for humanity. Why? Because all the obstacles to living out the missional truth have been removed. This is why I contend that sometimes, church leaders make a mistake pulling new believers away from comfortable settings where they believe and love their mission. We plug them in to uncomfortable ministry positions that keeps them busy doing church stuff. Eugene Peterson said it best when he said, "No matter how right we are in what we believe about God, no matter how accurately we phrase our belief or how magnificently and persuasively we preach or write or declare it, if love does not shape the way we speak and act, we falsify the creed, we confess a lie. Believing without loving is what gives religion a bad name." [10]

In a recent study published in May 2005 by Dr. Thom S. Rainer, Dean of the Billy Graham School at Southern Baptist Theological Seminary in Louisville, Kentucky, contends that while the "conservative resurgence" of the last 30 years has certainly transformed the Southern Baptist Convention into a more theologically and biblical body, it has failed to attract new followers. He writes:

"The Southern Baptist Convention (16 million members) is less evangelistic today than it was in the years preceding the conservative resurgence. We must conclude that the evangelistic growth of the denomination is stagnant, and that the onset of the conservative resurgence has done nothing to improve the trend of the number of annual baptisms which have remained unchanged since the 1950s." [11]

First love or creedal love as Eugene Peterson would call it, must be *"with all your heart, with all your mind, with all your soul, and with all your strength" (Mark 12:30 RSV).* This undergirds everything we do. *First* loving is not something we do after we have learned all the "basics." Instead, we must have this first internalized then missionalized as a way of life.[12]

What God desires most is the humanization of man, not the ritualization of religion. He wants us to live humanely and in gratitude, but we please him equally as much when we join him in his redemptive concern. For example, Jesus told us how we do for others and in a religious sense, we have done the act for God. When we feed the hungry, clothe the naked, give drink to the thirsty, and do any of this for the least among us, we do something also for God. After all, God's favorite charity is the human race. We make him happiest when we give to it. *"You shall love your neighbor as yourself" (Mark 12:31 RSV).*

How the church becomes distracted

Contemplate a total surrender of meaningless activities and church busyness. Let me ask. What would the church look like if we stopped counting people, stopped soliciting new donors, and stopped staffing or funding ministry programs that serve only our members? Reggie McNeal is bold and correct when he says, "The target of most church ministry efforts has been on the church itself and church members. Just look at how the money is spent and what the church leadership spends time doing. We have already rehearsed the poor return on investment we are seeing for this focus. …In the future the church that 'gets it' will staff to and spend its resources on strategies for community transformation."[13] Many of us in the church think people are looking only for something to believe in. This kind of thinking represents the former culture.

Distracted Churches: Identified by What They Do Not What They Say They Are

Figure 1 shows a list of distracted churches and their multiple functions. More significant than the list itself is the role of the local pastor and leaders and the corresponding role of church members. The role of the pastor, particularly, and his primary functions are like pieces of a pie when halved, quartered, and sliced even less. How the people see the pastor's pie (his activity not intentions) is the way the church will be and its membership. For instance, if the pastor expends most of his energies emphasizing the need for more workers to begin and sustain church programs, it can easily be interpreted as an organization primarily concerned about providing benefits. Thus, the pastor is the recruiter and the members are clubbers.

Closer examination of Figure 1 shows that all churches are listed. However, the church itself is not characterized as one type and not the others. In fact, most churches have most of these types and at least two of them. In other words, most churches are a combination of the characteristics listed. Critical to understanding distracted churches is being able to definitely describe where your church is located on the scale. Then, strategize ways to lead the church to practically demonstrate first love.

In the following pages of this chapter let's look at the impact of distracted churches. I hope you find it interesting.

DISTRACTED CHURCHES Chart		
Distracted Churches	**Role of Pastor and Church Leaders**	**Role of Church Members**
Missionary Church	Capital Fundraiser	Givers
Maintenance (Survivor) Church	Recruiter	Clubbers
Seeker-Sensitive Church (Weekend Church)	Presenter/Motivator	Seekers
Consumer Church	Producers	Consumers
Church Growth Church	Programmer/Assimilator Analysts	Participants
Activist Church	Catalyst	Activists

The Impact of the Missionary Church

This type of church is noted for sending a lot of missionaries to foreign countries, raising funds for missionaries, holding missions conferences and featuring missionaries prominently in the Sunday services when they are in town.

In his book *Church Next*, Eddie Gibbs made a similar observation on missions. He writes: "The majority of church leaders throughout the Western world find themselves ministering in a rapidly changing cultural context that is both post-Christian and pluralistic. Consequently, their outreach ministries are as cross-cultural as those of their more traditional missionary counterparts seeking to make Christ known in other parts of the world. Consequently they are in as much need of missionary training to venture across the street as to venture overseas."[14]

The Impact of the Maintenance-Survivor Church

Reggie McNeal describes these churches with a "club" mentality. They are churches who have made themselves their purpose. Their priorities include maintaining established programs and practices, in large part because they are established, and keeping people coming to the church in order to maintain the programs. The church building (enlarging and maintaining it) is often a key goal or priority.

This model easily surrenders to legalism and making a "little big horn" stand against the different look and change in the religious landscape. Many Christians who are loyal to this model see their faith and way of "doing" church as the only way. Tolerance of examining one's faith is seen as compromise of their interpretation of the Bible. Either/or answers are viewed as the right answers. Command and control are central issues in their view of church behavior. Discernment of scriptures, in their view, always runs consistent with church polity and doctrine. To them it would be reprehensible to question the way a church does things or gets things done. In their eyes, there is no middle ground to those who see their mission in life as preserving the church against the attacks of the world. The huge problem with this mentality is that the church is certainly not a perfect world to be in itself. Nor is it immune to human depravity. Consider the fallout of the Ted Haggard story that broke in early November in 2006.

The Impact of the Seeker-Sensitive Weekend Service Church

Over the last ten years especially, the burden of evangelism has shifted to the church service as a means of promoting the gospel.

The seeker model of ministry puts the major focus or emphasis of mission on what happens at a church during its weekend services. The objective for many worship teams is to provide experience via music, ambiance and theatre. In many churches, this model has proven successful in terms of increased attendance and assimilating people into the church service who were previously unchurched. However, one of the daggers of this approach has been a shift of responsibility to the programmatic aspect of the church service and an emphasis on invitational outreach. Less emphasis is placed on each individual follower of Jesus to live a life of discipleship that models the love and care that can attract unchurched people to the gospel. Another danger is the self-imposed pressure to out-perform, and out-experience the last worship performance. Sadly, when this occurs, the worship of creating worship happens.

In the reality show *American Choppers*, a highly motivated, boisterous father and his two sons make elaborate bikes or motorcycles. These customized bikes sell for $100,000 or more to their customers. Their business *Orange County Choppers* is based in Orange County, California.

With each episode, these creative bike builders start from scratch with nothing but chrome, sheet metal, nuts and bolts. With their expert welding, they fashion some of the most beautiful machines you have ever seen. It is absolutely incredible to see these choppers up on blocks. Before the finished product hits the street for a test run, these artists shine it, put fuel in it, listen to the motor run, and stand back and admire their work. Interestingly, while the bike still sets up on blocks, it logs no miles, it does not go away, it does not help anyone and essentially, it is nothing more than a collectible. The true purpose of it all is not accomplished until a satisfied customer purchases the cycle and hits the road.

In a very real sense, we sometimes allow the church to rest "up on blocks." As leaders, we shine it with our attractive bulletins, put fuel in it with our slick marketing, and listen to the engine run with our smoothly orchestrated services while every member is busy working in the church. To us, the church becomes a thing of beauty to be admired when we say, "We have a good church."

However, unless our church is "off the blocks" and hitting the streets, then it records no missional miles, it does not help the unchurched, and it becomes nothing more than a collectible where consistent Sunday tours occur. If our church is not showing wear and tear, then we have abandoned our *first* love and the missional transformation is absent.

The Impact of the Consumer Church

Appropriately named, the church becomes a vendor of religious goods and services. People are attracted to the church to be fed and to have their needs met. The major emphasis is to "go" or "come" to the church. Programs and ministries are more attractional than incarnational. This explains why the church talks less about spirituality and more about announcements, prayer requests, and the like. It is all about having what people want so they come to the church as a consumer. However, this comfort and satisfaction is dangerous. The consumer Christian finds what they believe they need and the church gets to count heads.

While surfing, I came across an article published by a spiritual blogger name Jason Zahariades. When I first read his comments, I immediately knew he had said something profound. In his article *Detoxing from Church*, Zahariades discusses the impact consumerism is having on the American church. This blogger used the metaphor of being "addicted" to church and the painful detoxing process a person would experience if they stripped away their connection to the organizational church and examined the non-authenticity and impotence of their own faith. He writes:

> "In the Americanized church, the organization is designed to turn life and faith into a simple prepackaged consumer product.... Remember, we must **leave** the church in order to BE the Church. We must stop being churched and start being the Church.
>
> ...A primary difference between being churched and being the Church is how I approach the community. Being

churched assumes the organizational church is designed from the perspective that I am a consumer of religious goods and services. Therefore, I am expected to participate in the church's programs chiefly to receive and consume."[15]

We must remember that meeting needs does not satisfy needs. Rather, it raises the consumerism in all of us to view the church as responsible for our own spiritual and personal growth issues. Soon we become immature, undiscipled Christians who have not discovered the joy of knowing God's strength for living and the real change that occurs from a genuine, consistent, intimate relationship with Christ.

Once we understand what it means to be the people of God and to shoulder our responsibility for personal transformation into Christlikeness, then we are better able to see Christian community. By doing this, Christ, instead of the church, fills all the needs for our lives as we follow in accordance to 2 Peter 1:3 and not by participating in and consuming church programs. Then, this inner transformation of doing the words and deeds of Christ are not the focus but the natural outcome or by-product.

It would actually be healthy for some of us who are addicted consumers of the church to be detoxed by going "cold turkey." At least for a few Sundays. "Why such drastic measures? Involvement in an organizational consumer-driven church blinds us to the real state of our lives. By participating in this kind of church I can enjoy inspiring worship, biblical exposition of Scripture, fellowship, small groups, kids programs, service projects, missions, discipleship, books, radio broadcasts, multimedia presentations and virtually anything else I need in my spiritual life. In fact, I can enjoy an entirely alternative lifestyle where Christianity is prepackaged for me—books, music, entertainment, new reports, advice, etc. And as I consume it, if forms a façade over the real condition of my life. The rub is when my true condition actually bubbles to the surface and I find myself troubled, discontent or miserable. Then the church or the pastor or the worship team has lost the 'anointing' and I must find a new organizational church that will provide me what I need to feel better about who I am." [16]

"It's no longer merely about size, seeker sensitivity, spiritual gifts, church health, nor the number of small groups. It's about making a significant and sustainable difference in the lives of people around us—in our communities and in our cities. As we enter the third Millennium, the church of North America faces the opportunity to once again become a positive force for change."

Eric Swanson, Leadership Network

Have you ever borrowed a book and failed to return it? If so, I should know about you. One of my biggest pet peeves (and we all have them) is loaning a book to someone who forgets to give it back. Maybe it is because I love books so much. Most of the time, it is not that at all. There is much more. Truthfully speaking, I miss hearing how that person enjoyed the book or received insights from it. To me, that is the reward for loaning books. It is not sharing the book, but rather sharing the experience of the book. When someone fails to return the book, the circle of sharing is incomplete.

I have the same response when loaning or borrowing garden tools, wrenches, screwdrivers, and the like. But what if we use borrowed tools not suited for us or for our situation? Now that is a different matter. Do we try to make them work like the proverbial saying, "putting a square peg into a round hole" before we give in and admit we are using the wrong tools? Sometimes, our frustration leads us to continue to work harder using borrowed tools not suited for the task, yet expecting different results. Sound familiar?

Consequently, the church of North America recognizes the complexity of our times but seems unwilling at this point to acknowledge its own cultural imprisonment.

A steroid Christianity all muscled up with multi-sensory, high-tech, high-powered worship on Sundays is not enough. People ask, "Is it real or is it steroid?" People are hungering to taste an authentic encounter with the Spirit of God.

Ann Siddall, who has written a timely article about the spirituality revolution occurring in the West, cautions the church and encourages a change in behavior. "This is not a time for brooding over our failures, or trying to put into place programs and plans that will 'get people back'. It is a time for deep prayer and reflection, as we struggle against the temptations to become successful and powerful, and try to listen for the invitations of the Spirit and to understand how God is self-revealing in our time." Siddall insists, "There is not going to be a quick or easy transition from the church of yesterday to the church of tomorrow. It is a time when deep listening and waiting are required, a time for risking things, for not being able to guarantee results, for giving without counting the cost and without binding ourselves up with the need to produce outcomes." [17]

The Impact of the Church-Growth Church

In this chapter we will discuss how Church Growth Movement of the 70s and 80s, consumerism, and other overused approaches to "doing" church are in essence deviations of the gospel. They serve as unreturned, borrowed tools, which have led the church to doing time. In contrast, these once viewed blessings of the church have now reversed themselves to become impediments to church members. In fact, church alumni and the unchurched want their "spirituality to be connected to daily life, to scientific discovery, to their workplace, to mental and physical well-ness, and to a lifestyle that may not include institutional religion."[18]

In his book *A Life with Purpose*, George Mair tells the history of how the "model of the Church Growth Movement was to move away from the model of a small, traditional congregation of five hundred or so lifelong churchgoers."[19] Mair also declares that the goal of this new model for the church is to "operate on a more massive scale, striving to attract thousands of unchurched men and women and introduce them to Jesus. In 1979, the year before Rick Warren started the Saddleback Valley Community Church, there were ten mega churches in the United States. The next year, the total leapt to fifty, and ten years later, in 1990, it had grown to three hundred churches. By 1999, there were five hundred mega churches in the country. Today, more than 1.7 million Protestants in America attend mega churches. Not surprisingly, many of those men and women are concentrated in Southern California, which had a particularly large population of unchurched people....The numbers speak for themselves. The Church Growth Movement has been wildly successful in Southern California, as well as in the rest of the country." [20]

A humorous story emerged recently on the internet among church emailers. It is called *The Squirrels* and the author is unknown. It goes like this. "Three churches in town were overrun with squirrels. After much prayer, the elders of the first church determined that the animals were predestined to be there. Who were they to interfere with God's will? They did nothing, and the squirrels multiplied. The elders of the second church, deciding that they could not harm any of God's creatures, humanely trapped the squirrels and then set them free outside of town. Three days later, the squirrels were back. It was only the third church that succeeded in keeping the squirrels away. The elders of this church simply baptized the squirrels and registered them as members of the church. Now, they only see the squirrels on Christmas and Easter.

In a similar way, anyone who has attended church for a while knows this fictional squirrel story characterizes the modern church. Has the Church Growth Movement redirected American adults back to the church?

Barna states, "Despite widespread efforts to increase church attendance across the nation, the annual survey of church attendance conducted by The Barna Group shows that one-third of all adults (34%) remain unchurched. That proportion has changed little during the past five years. However, because of the nation's population continuing growth, the number of unchurched adults continues to grow by nearly a million people annually." [21]

Unquestionably, modernity poses problems for the church-growth movement and does much damage to faith itself. Guinness contends, "America's crisis of cultural authority and the global challenge of modernity provide the setting and underscore the significance of the church-growth movement and the megachurches. To be sure, many church-growth advocates see the church's problem simply as a matter of out-of-date structures and out-of-touch communication, which can all be remedied easily. This naiveté' trivializes a crisis that is far more massive than they realize. But it is not surprising that when the church, and its ministers and their preaching, are all widely perceived as irrelevant in the modern world, such a resort to new forms of authority and relevance appears justified as well as necessary."[22]

What is Guinness actually saying? Guinness is cautioning the North American church as it slips into the clutches of the church-growth movement, which is a by-product of the secularization in America by its obsessions with the exaltation of numbers and of technique. Both of these obsessions are very prominent in the church-growth movement. Church leaders have become fascinated with statistics, data, and marketing concepts In other words, we have rationalized that religious ideas are less meaningful and our religious institutions are less influential because of the advances of modernity in the late twentieth century. What was once left to God and human participation under the leadership of God are now classified calculated and controlled by the systematic application of reason and technique. Like the business world, the church is conscious of its target audience, periods of receptivity, trends, efficiency, quantifiability, productivity, and of course the grander use of technology.

Modernity convinced us of our need to become up to date or modern. Supposedly, the decline in church attendance across America was because our churches were too small, relied too heavily on the "one size fits all" concept, and missed numerous opportunities to market itself to a more professional, sophisticated public. Now, as one who formerly bought into the systems and concepts of the Church Growth Movement, I am left with more questions about the condition of the North American church culture. For example, if Barna's 2005 research is correct, (I have no reason to believe otherwise) then, how is it that the number of adults who are unchurched in this country has changed little in the last five years? Why hasn't the gap closed? Does the church-growth movement promote an emphasis on "servicing the self" instead of serving God? Have leaders viewed Church Growth as a science with predictable results? Will the megachurch model of catering (like a shopping mall) to the needs of people turnaround small and mid-size churches? As church leaders, have we traded in faithfulness to God's Word, godly deeds and godly behavior for a successful church?

As one can see, I have listed many questions. However, in this chapter I would like to address three key questions that strike at the heart of validity within the Church Growth Movement.

They are:

1. *Has the obsession to be acclaimed a "growing church" much as we would herald a growing business in the eyes of the public, actually shifted the focus of churches and denominations away from simply "being the church"?*
2. *Will the replication and refinement of more church-growth principles satisfy our culture's hunger for the Spirit?*
3. *In the future, will today's teenagers, whom Barna calls the "mosaics" evolve back to pre-church-growth movement ideals and desire a more apostolic missionary church in quest for a genuine expression of spirituality?*

When a church focuses on trying to grow, the larger mission suffers and the church can actually become less attractive. The major deficiency of the church-growth movement is this obsession by church leaders to be classified as a "growing church" among their peers within the Christian community. Being awarded as a growing congregation starts the ball rolling. Modernity has convinced the public that any church like any business has no significance or reason for existence unless it is growing or increasing in size. Consequently, added pressure is placed upon every church to increase in size because there is less loyalty to a particular church or affiliation and more "church shopping" practiced by church attenders. The downside of this deficiency is that a church can never assume it has assimilated its members or be able to know just when the leadership no longer has to worry about their attendance and institutional support. The problem today is that too many churches and denominations have focused on declining statistical reports and have focused on defending their title like a sports team hoping to defend its previous championship. Instead, shouldn't the church desire most to win another "championship" for God by seeing authentic revival and renewal to "be the church" rather than "doing church."?

What are the alternatives? Let us first begin by making some admissions. Church Growth is not a theology and certainly not an exact science. Further, like many movements, the church-growth movement is a mixture of things good, bad, and in-between. Staying abreast with church-growth terms such as "niche marketing," audience-driven," "purpose-driven," seeker-friendly," "full-service churches," and the "homogeneous unit principle," can bother your mind and interrupt your relationship with the Almighty.

According to Rainer, "Church growth, historically understood and properly defined, is simply *evangelism* that results in the growth of the church. Yet the perception today seems to be that church growth is concerned about the absolute size of the church regardless of the type of growth. We who identify ourselves with church growth should recognize that the movement is in an identity crisis because of lack of clarity in our purpose. Our critics are not at fault when they misunderstand us, mislabel us, and misapply our principles. So much takes place under the guise of church growth that it should not surprise us when our purpose is misunderstood. Let's learn from our critics. If they do not understand us, let us have greater and more specific clarity in our purpose." [23]

After hearing these admissions, I would listen to what the culture is saying about the church itself becoming too much like a business. Have you attended a church worship service so technologically driven, so artistically choreographed, so time-conscious, and so "machine-like" that you actually catch yourself wishing for more spontaneity, more human error and best of all an interruption by the Spirit of God? I quiet often do.

To me, there seems to be some traction for the impromptu, the spontaneity, and the opportunity for those who are marginalized by education and social status to be allowed to participate in worship. Perhaps it is the perception that more God and Spirit authenticity is present when all types of human participants with their human errors are accepted—not just the technological errors or the errors of those identified as "spiritually gifted" in a certain way. Sometimes I think we go through this whole "spiritual-gift analysis" thing to help leaders enlist volunteers to do the jobs (sometimes ministries) of the church and to keep the church (machine) propped up and going.

Moreover, reaching for the "growing church" label can become idolatrous. Noted theologian Os Guinness thinks so. "In the case of the church-growth movement, this idolizing trend can develop in one of two ways: either the insights and tools of modernity are themselves relied upon idolatrously, or the churches themselves become idolatrous because their very success as institutions makes them into an end in themselves." [24]

My second question zeroes in on the heart and validity of the Church Growth Movement. *Will the replication and refinement of more church-growth principles satisfy our culture's hunger for the Spirit?*

Interestingly, at one time in my ministry I would have agreed with most church-growth principles and the results they predicted. However, today I am rethinking those same principles.

Nancy Pearcy writes, "If Christians do not develop their own tools of analysis, then when some issue comes up that they want to understand, they'll reach over and borrow someone else's tools—whatever concepts are generally accepted in their professional field or in the culture at large." [25]

The problem when Christians borrow tools, Os Guinness points out, that they do not realize that "they are borrowing not an isolated tool but a whole philosophical toolbox laden with tools which have their own particular bias to every problem. Using tools of analysis that have non-Christian assumptions embedded in them is like wearing someone else's glasses or walking in someone else's shoes." [26]

Borrowed tools capture the user, who then fails to be salt and light. Unfortunately, this is what many of us do. We stuff our toolboxes with a combination of both the secular and the sacred. It is only later that we discover, attached like a sticky note to each secular tool used, a philosophical drift from the Bible. If we are not careful, we become obsessed with the tool and forget the Power to use the tool.

For example, due to increased federal pressure for better performance, schools are tempted to teach to raise their test scores instead of teaching for the benefit of the child. In a similar way, the church often yields to the temptation of becoming obsessed with the mechanics of church growth and this whole idea of being a "growing church" while glibly celebrating the immeasurable, joyous aspects of God changing lives both spiritually and culturally.

The Impact of the Activist Church

In the weeks leading up to the 2004 presidential election I anxiously followed the news of the growing numbers of Christian conservatives nationwide who were being targeted and mobilized by talk-show radio hosts and parachurch organizations to become political activists. To my surprise, the intensity and the activism of the movement came to my own church. One beautiful fall Sunday Morning, the church greeter welcomed me to church wearing conspicuous stickers supporting his presidential candidate of choice on both lapels of his gray pin-stripped suit. Immediately, I winced, took the Sunday bulletin from his hand, and went inside. At 51, as a minister for 35 years and someone who had been in rural Baptist churches all his life, I was appalled and outraged at what I had just seen. With the exception of a handful of people, I felt violated, pressured, and marginalized and I am a conservative myself. Some questions came to mind. How many visitors from the community will show up at our church and turn away, offended by my friend's activism? Does my friend and others really believe their political activism is evangelism? If so, is the church dangerously outsourcing its evangelistic opportunities by taking this controversial stance?

Consequently, religious fervor has been used for a political home field advantage. Political voices have found that persisting with certain social issues provides them a huge political advantage. Not even with control in the all three branches of government have abortion, gay marriage and stem-cell research been legislatively reversed as promised in previous campaign rhetoric. On-going social issues possess the power to drive some folks away from the voting booth and others to it. Self-deception is like this. It blinds us to the true cause of problems and then we offer solutions that make matters worse. To the extent that the church is always standing up against issues, we are always flirting with the idolatrous self-delusion which prevents faithful discipleship.For nearly forty years, church members continually asked one another "Where were all the Christians when the church needed them the most especially when women were given the right to choose in the monumental *Roe v.*

Wade court ruling of 1973?" As a result, the abortion issue remains the ardent mission of conservative evangelicals today.

Undoubtedly, the American church retains enormous guilt for her silence and apathy in the political process after federal courts gave women the right to choose. The 40,000 or so abortions that occurred every year thereafter have moved those guilt feelings into political activism.

The 2004 electoral map was a sea of Republican red, with islands of Democratic blue in the Northeast, upper Midwest and West Coast. George W. Bush was re-elected for a second term by a record of nearly 120 million voters.

More than 23 million evangelical Christians flocked to the polls and cast their vote for moral values. When asked about the issues affecting their vote exit polls of Americans revealed that 22 percent said moral values were most important to them. Moral values were more important than terrorism, the war in Iraq, heath care and other domestic issues.

Evangelical Christians seemed to have been more than outraged. They seemed to have carried with them an aura of righteous indignation and anger, stomping their feet and vowing to "take America back." Many of the evangelical Christian community blame themselves for not being political in the 1960s and 1970s when the prayer in school debate, and most importantly the abortion issue were decided. They had seen enough. In the end, the nation polarized sharply over the mixing of religion and politics. Many Christians believe they have made a difference. Others disagree.

In her most recent book *It's My Party Too*, Christine Todd Whitman describes religious leaders as "…no longer content to save souls one by one through the work of their churches. They set their sights higher, with their self-described mission being to save the nation's soul through its political institutions, using civil law to impose religious law." [27]

While abortion is clearly wrong and homosexuality is a practice condemned in the Bible, the church can ill afford to shift its message from one of redemption and hope for humanity to a message of activism alone. Just think how terrible it would be if religious institutions carried labels of red and blue churches and the membership requirements included a litmus test concerning your political persuasion. Churches would have to be selective in the hiring of a pastor. In turn, pastors would not be eligible for some pastorates. Is this what we want to happen in America?

Unless North American church culture defuses the polarized political thinking prevalent today, we will hear of incidents of dismissed church members because they do not vote for a particular political candidate. Is this what we want to happen in America?

Interestingly, not all Americans, not all Christians and certainly not all evangelicals believe saving the nation's soul by putting all their eggs into one basket is a viable answer. In her book *Total Truth*, Nancy Pearcy, describes evangelicals as eager for change. She writes, "They leaped into political activism as the quickest, surest way to make a difference in the public arena—failing to realize that politics tends to reflect culture, not the other way around."[28]

Once, Pearcy recalled a discussion with the Bill Wichterman, policy advisor to Senate Majority Leader Bill Frist. "We have learned that politics is downstream from culture, not the other way around. Real change has to start with the culture. All we can do on Capitol Hill is to try to find ways government can nurture healthy cultural trends." [29]

So, how does all this shake out for the church? Politicians cannot and will not de-polarize the church's political paralysis. The church must escape captivity by returning to her mission.

Is the calling of every Christian to fulfill God's higher calling to reform culture within their own circles of influence such as their families, schools, churches, workplaces, neighborhoods, health clubs, and civic organizations?

Consider for a moment that, as Christians we admit we have lost the culture because of our reluctance, hesitance, or whatever it might be, failing to engage this biblically illiterate and Christless society. Is it because we do not understand humanity today and therefore opting for political activism and to bullhorn people instead? Has our frustration with the moral decline of the last fifty years forced us to cave in to waging a culture war using the world's weapons and methods as our own?

More questions. "Will there be a price for the church to pay for being joined at the hip with the political system?" If so, what will it be? Does morality come by changing the laws of the land and prescribed viewpoints, or is the heart of an individual changed by the presence of Christ one person at a time? Further, how has the church accomplished her ecclesiastical mission up to this time? Is Acts 1:8 enough? Alternatively, does the church need a bigger bull-horn? Has the church been captured by a socialist separate movement within a political party whose true motives and global agenda have yet to be disclosed? More importantly, how are church leaders treating each other these days? If churches participate more in the political process, will the church excuse itself from engaging the world (culture) through relationships? Is saving the nation's soul the single mission of the church or only the result of authentic change in the people by the transforming power and presentation of Christ's message through the scriptures?

The Missional Reality

It may not sound obvious to improve first love among distracted churches. But this is precisely what should occur. We desperately need to focus on the missional realities rather than our intentions. Yet it is surprising how little we do in this practice. I have listened to hundreds of church pastors and leaders use the principle of self-learning and planning and somehow prefer to ignore reality.

Focusing on missional realities, however, immediately creates energy in our minds. We open up ideas and possibilities. If we want our church transformed and our people to return to their first love, we want them focused on their missional reality most of the time. This does not mean we do not plan ahead—far from it; it means we address our situation by analyzing the way forward, instead of the causes. Let me illustrate this with the following examples:

MISSIONAL REALITIES CHART								
		Missionary Church	Maintenance (Survivor) Church	Seeker-Sensitive Church (Weekend Church)	Consumer Church	Church Growth Church	Activist Church	Missional Church
THE FIVE TRANSFORMING STEPS	Missional Spirituality–The Soul's Passion	The passion for recognition is greater than the passion for Kingdom work.	The spirituality is to remain solvent in ministry, to maintain the what already exists.	The spirituality is to introduce missionaries to the worship for exposure.	The spirituality is primarily derived from the spirituality of the leader.	The passion for numbers if greater than the passion for kingdom work.	The spiritual passion is take our country back by taking a political stance.	The spirituality is reclaiming our first love for God and humanity.
	Missional Calling–The Soul's Formation	Recruitment of volunteers is designed to build mission support.	The primary mission connection is through prayer.	The calling is to attract more people.	The identity is fuzzy and the goal is to produce goods and services that meet needs.	The calling is to develop a growing - church reputation.	The calling is to react to cultural issues.	The missional calling is to see ourselves as missionaries in our homes, schools, workplace and neighborhoods.
	Missional Visioning–The Soul's Dwelling	Viewing the church as doing missions but not seeing ourselves (as individuals) as missionaries	Having a missions committee keeps the people informed of prayer concerns and needs.	The vision is to participate and experience.	The vision breaks down when the leader's vision blurs.	The vision provides the programs to increase assimilation and member involvement.	The vision is to roll back cultural changes to an era more receptive to the church.	The missional vision is to make disciples who understand the culture and join spiritual conversations.
	Missional Learning–The Soul Living Free	The learning lens gives a view of how others are doing mission and the church can join that effort.	The learning is for information not for transformation. The learning is an "end" and not a "means".	The learning modality is glamorous and entertaining.	The learning is limited to what leaders know and disseminate.	The learning is how to interpret and manipulate groups, subsets of people, and trends.	The learning is designed to catapult the members into a political stance, grand standing before the community.	The people are salt and light to every generation. The gospel is not selective of its audience. The church is relevant and engaging to the culture.
	Missional Accountability–The Soul's Transformation	Every member is motivated to support missions due to guilt.	Every member pays dues and receives benefits from the club.	Every member looks for a new adventure through worship.	Every member is dependent on the paid staff.	Every member a minister.	Every member agrees with the stance of the church.	Every member a missionary.

Looking at the Missional Realities Chart, notice how church members are released to view their workplaces, homes, schools, and neighborhoods as their mission. Isn't this a biblical reality too?

The Biblical Reality

Both John the Baptist and Jesus were strongly influenced in their eschatological views by Isaiah the Prophet. Without hesitation, they *"prepared the way of the Lord…a highway for our God"* (Isaiah 40:3 RSV) as their mission. Jesus' efforts were to set free the captives (most of them religious) from their religiosity and legalism.

Isaiah 40-55 was written to a people in Babylonian exile or captivity (sixth century B.C.). These writings were first called "The Exile's Book of Consolations." They were a series of proclamations announcing Jerusalem's deliverance from her "warfare" (Isaiah 40:2 RSV) or time of service. The nation Israel had lost everything. They lost their country, their Temple, and their families. Their leaders had been scattered, and occasionally, a messenger would bring more bad news. They questioned God's interest in them and even his whereabouts. The exiles had great difficulty in believing Yahweh had any control over what went on in the world. In turn, they questioned why He was allowing them to languish in captivity without any indication of His presence.

Many of their children married foreigners, embracing strange new gods, while the old traditional views were in danger of being lost forever. They had doubts about God, themselves, and about the future that looked so bleak. They were in Babylon captivity and needed freedom.

Their difficulties were physical, political, cultural, and geographical. Israel was doing time for mixing their activities and merging their beliefs with the worldview prevalent in that day. They had stopped spreading the message of Yahweh and the idea of monotheism by no longer confronting the foreign gods of other nations. Instead, they allowed themselves to be influenced and ruled because they forgot their monotheistic worship of God and their responsibility to be the leader of God's mission to the nations. After all, God's missionary concern for the exiles was that their role and especially their mission reflected His purpose to all mankind. Isaiah 43:10-13 RSV reflects this missionary motif as a strong feature of God's plans and purposes.

"You are my witnesses, says the Lord, and my servant whom I have chosen, that you may know and believe me and understand that I am He. Before me no god was formed, nor shall there be any after me. I am the Lord, and besides me there is no savior. I declared and saved and proclaimed, where there was no strange god among you; and you are my witnesses, says the Lord. I am God, and also henceforth I am He; there is none who can deliver from my hand; I work and who can hinder it?"

Although geography revealed no giant peaks or deep ravines between Babylon and Jerusalem, these mountains and chasms were in their heads and in their hearts. They had to get up the nerve to leave the comfort of captivity to go home.

Enter the prophet Isaiah. He knew their condition and their mindset. He began in Isaiah 40 with words of comfort or encouragement.

"A voice cries: In the desert prepare the way of the Lord, Make straight in the desert a highway for our God. Every valley shall be lifted up, every mountain and hill be made low; the uneven ground shall become level, the rough places a plain." (Isaiah 40:3-4 RSV)

In short, Isaiah helped the people to see that God was where they were and that God had not forgotten them. Their captivity was mostly in their heads and in their hearts. By returning to the original mission given to them by God, they found forgiveness and restoration.

The Bible tells us that Jesus read from Second Isaiah, the prophesy of his own mission to his culture. "*The scroll of the prophet Isaiah was handed to him. Unrolling it, he found the place where it is written: The Spirit of the Lord is on me, because he has anointed me to preach good news to the poor. He has sent me to proclaim freedom for the prisoners and recovery of sight for the blind, to release the oppressed, to proclaim the year of the Lord's favor" (Luke 4:17-19 NIV).*

Interestingly, Jesus began his earthly ministry (missional reality) by offering individuals freedom from the trappings of institutional religion and later prayed in John 17 for his disciples and for all future believers to engage the world with the same mission. After Pentecost, the Spirit became the continuing presence of Christ. Jesus prayed:

"I am coming to you now, but I say these things while I am still in the world, so that they may have the full measure of my joy within them. I have given them your word and the world has hated them, for they are not of the world any more than I am of the world... As you sent me into the world, I have sent them into the world....I pray also for those who believe in me through their message, that all of them may be one, Father, just as you are in me and I am in you. May they also be in us so that the world may believe that you sent me" (John 17:13-20 NIV).

The Jewish people of Jesus' day had a political agenda to get their country back. As a result of what their religion had become in the days of Isaiah, they lost their nation and land to ungodly influences. Still, hundreds of years later, they were praying for God to give back their country but did not recognize Jesus the Christ when He was among them. They called Him a blasphemer.

One of the enduring tensions of figuring out church is how to be in the world yet not of it. As church leaders, we have overlooked that the primary place where missional encounter takes place is in the world. And, the church has done little to equip its members to be missional.

James Emery White, author of *Serious Times*, questions the church's ability to be the church. Like others, he too looked at the church and all he could see was a stagnant, graying organization reluctant to be cutting edge. Unfortunately, this is all too normal in our church culture today. White suggests:

The church must be restored to its rightful place in our thought and lives and rethought in terms of mission effectiveness. Doing this will demand scrutinizing tired methods, inane traditions and outmoded approaches to outreach. Unfortunately, even broaching this subject is confusing to many Christians.

Those who write the most about addressing our culture tend to set up contemporary approaches to ministry as their favorite straw man to knock down (as some, the real culture war is not between a Christian worldview and secularization but between organs and drums, liturgy and PowerPoint. This reveals a tragic inability to see the heart of the issue, which effectively marginalizes the church. As things now stand, many Christians never darken the church's doorway (or take its efforts seriously) because of tired, dilapidated wineskins. Denounced as selling out to culture are those who attempt to return to a cutting-edge ministry on the frontline of kingdom advance. This stalemate must be breached. [30]

This book will help readers examine why we should not use the works of the flesh to accomplish the works of the Spirit as a central part of our own theology and everyday practice. I am not suggesting that religion does not have a place in politics. Nor am I advocating not discussing the two in the same breathe. However, I am suggesting the North American church is distracted and most of us know it if we are honest about it.

The tragedy of September 11 showed us the importance of religion in our country when public prayers occurred in any public place and no one objected. We must never forget how genuine faith in God can influence our priorities and practices. Yet, we are not immune to distractions.

So, what is my point? As Christians, we need to develop belief systems that examine the influence of religion on politics and social reform without getting into bed with a particular political party and running the risk of being used for votes and knowing that you are being used for an entire gamut of other reasons.

Jim Wallis, author of *God's Politics* says, "We should talk less about the ideological categories of Left and Right, and more about what kind of people we want to be, what kind of community, what kind of world. Even those who do not trust organized religion often do want to talk about spiritual or moral values. Applying spiritual values to politics will be the key." [31]

In our efforts to change America, we have unleashed the demons of in-house turmoil and marginalization of our own. Christians have resorted to "fighting fire with fire" by telling other Christians they cannot be a Christian if they vote a particular political persuasion. To me, this shows how we can deceive ourselves. We will all get burned in this process!

Denominations, state conventions, associations, and local churches in the direct jet stream flow of parachurch organizations with political agendas subtly drift off course. Two years ago, I sat in an associational meeting of Baptist churches and watched church leaders fight among themselves. There were present those peace-makers who tried to find the common ground, but neither side would hear of it. It was all or nothing at all. In the end, a successful pastor and his congregation of 500 were out of fellowship with the other churches. The sad part is this. Most people in those churches do not want to see each other as the enemy. All they want is a place to worship their God and be on mission. And you can believe that the real Enemy has scored the biggest victory of them all.

Chapter Two

THE THREE PRIMARY REALMS OF CHURCH: RELATIONAL, ORGANIZATIONAL, AND MISSIONAL

"The central problem of our age is not liberalism or modernism– The real problem is this: the church of the Lord Jesus Christ, individually or corporately, tending to do the Lord's work in the power of the flesh rather than of the Spirit. The central problem is always in the midst of the people of God, not in the circumstances surrounding them."

–Francis Schaeffer

Introduction

Interestingly, the animated movie *Madagascar* was a huge blockbuster in theaters during the Summer of 2005. The film's characters are Alex the Lion, Marty the Zebra, Gloria the Hippo, Melman the Giraffe and a trio of penguins. They all live lavish lives in captivity at the Central Park Zoo in New York. Born in the zoo, Alex the Lion lived a life of privilege but the king of the beast has been so long in the zoo he has forgotten how to roar. His problem is solved when the penguins plot to escape to Antarctica and solicit the company of their friends including Alex the Lion. Surprisingly, all the characters escape in wooden crates placed on a cargo ship. Later, they fall overboard and float to the exotic beaches of the island Madagascar. It is there, deep within the jungle, where Alex the Lion gets his roar back because he is being who God created him to be.

Like Alex the Lion, many churches have lost their roar. In our world of doing, we cannot be. So, we strive for busyness and usefulness and lose our being and mission. So, what is the church facing? The greatest challenge facing churches today is to get their "roar" back to quiet this world's jungle.

A Google Earth View From Above

For the North American church, the influences of postmodernity and relevance has a false allure that masks both its built-in transience and its catch-22 demand. When the church utilizes "borrowed" tools instead of the work of God's Spirit, it is like marrying the princess of the age but soon becoming a widower.

Church growth ideals and the need-meeting approach (consumerism Christianity) overlook certain things. First, there is no matching truth of Scripture for practicing with these "borrowed" tools. Secondly, it promotes an uncritical engagement with modernity. In the words of Scott Thomas, "The culture around us sees the church rather, as a blow-up doll bride. We have all been sent by God to go into our own city and communities as missionaries who are culturally entrenched and personally involved. We must incarnate Christ's life in order to impact this culture that is pagan in every way. The church exists to proclaim the gospel in a relational way to the lost by the power of the Holy Spirit."[1]

Acts 1:8, "But you shall receive power when the Holy Spirit has come upon you; and you shall be witnesses to Me in Jerusalem, and in all Judea and Samaria, and to the end of the earth."

While church culture is in solitary confinement, it is my sincere prayer that she will not seek deliverance from captivity by yet more modernity but instead will seek sensitivity to the presence of God and learn lessons He has for the church regardless of the pain it inflicts upon us as the Christian community.

The Bible tells us about the power of God, the power of truth, and the power of the gospel itself. *"For God did not give us a spirit of timidity, but a spirit of power, of love and of self-discipline*"(2 Timothy 2:13 NIV). In fact, the New Testament Greek word *dunamis* means "spiritual power." Even political power or moral power cannot standup to the power of God or his ways. So why do we place so much trust in man's methods and ways? If we believe that the gospel message is powerful, then why are we using the world's methods and the world's tools? Do the tools of church growth and modernity have a stranglehold on the church?

With competing voices clamoring to be heard, the church **can** develop missionary sensitivity to postmodern culture, vision, and practices, and engage in God's mission with the non-Christian culture around it. This new century has exposed the need for churches in North America to make organizational adjustments to maximize ministry effectiveness, intentionally develop relationships anchored in faith formation which produces genuine disciple-making, and to instinctively respond missionally to the spiritual questing that takes place everyday somewhere in our homes, schools, neighborhoods, coffee shops and workplaces.

The three primary realms of church ministry are relational, organizational, and missional. Most of us understand how at times one aspect needs to dominate. However, at other times, each aspect presents conflict with the other. Twentieth Century tools of modernity have taught the church well, especially when it comes to knowing how to live and function as an organization. Interestingly, many churches and their leaders now have an acute awareness about how they behave organizationally (almost unconsciously at times). By their own admissions and "leader talk", they seem to know how to make organizational adjustments and re-align their infrastructure so it better serves the effectiveness of ministry. This area is not difficult to change.

Additionally, church leaders are effectively leading their congregations to becoming more intentional and creative in their relationship building efforts. In the last decade, churches have made measurable progress in their treatment and assimilation of visitors by prioritizing relationship through small groups.

The Illusion of Being Missional

While many agree the North American church is doing quite well in the way it morphs relationally and organizationally, becoming missional will be far more difficult for two important reasons.

Most churches think they are in mission if they raise money for charity or try to influence public policy without thinking about how to make mission central to worship design or equip laity to do hands-on mission locally and globally.

To worship God with a missional perspective is to worship Him from the perspective of <u>being</u> a missionary. The classic example of this missional outlook that I am speaking of is illustrated in Paul's sermon at the Areopagus Meeting at Mars Hill recorded in Acts 17.

Paul was informed enough about the cultural secularism including their images, idols, and poets, that he could easily re-direct the philosophical conversations from appeasing false gods to proclaiming the sovereignty of God over all creation and of the one true God and his son Jesus. How could he do this? His missionary sensitivity was as natural as breathing in and out but not because he was commissioned as a missionary sent by the church. Instead, his missionary "sentness" came from God and his perspective came from his personal worship of the one true God and his familiarity with the world and its spiritual hunger.

The reality of being missional in worship design is all about rediscovering our abandoned love experienced and spoken of the church at Ephesus in Revelation 2:4 RSV.

I know your works, your toil and your patient endurance, and how you cannot bear evil men but have tested those who call themselves apostles but are not, and found them to be false; I know you are enduring patiently and bearing up for my name's sake, and you have not grown weary. But I have against you, that you have abandoned the love you had at first.

Too often, our worship is about ourselves with no real connection with the world people live in. We have all heard the pleas. "Do you have a job in the church? You're saved so you can work and serve in the church." When I hear those voices come from those who stand behind pulpits I want to scream, "Somebody help me escape from all this church stuff!" In other words, our corporate worship can become, and often is, a cultural life form that has carefully crafted and exported its own language, traditions, and rituals. Over time the songs, prayers, and routines become how worship is done.

The Organizational Realm of Church

Figure 1 below shows us the 20th century North American church in its current mindset and perspective *before* the world came to us to form a pluralistic society. Notice closely how the power of the corporateness of the church is illustrated here. At the center is the hub of ministry operations if you please.

The 20th Century Church
Figure 1

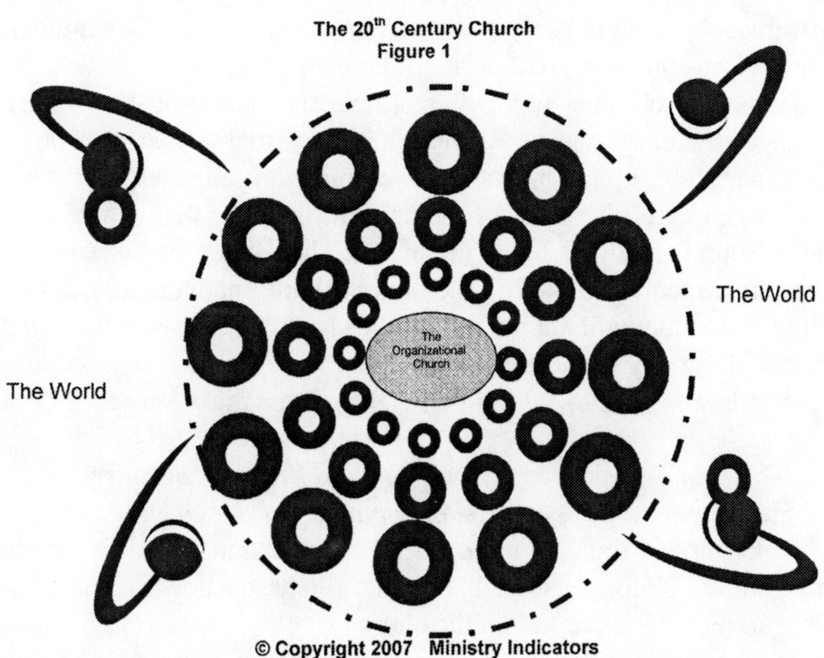

© Copyright 2007 Ministry Indicators

Notice The Organizational Hardwiring Of Many Churches Today

1. To attract people away from the world and offer a new world inside the walls of the church.

Organizational church is plagued with a superior attitude that reinforces the message of loyalty to the institution. Many of us have preached for years that the world is evil and the church is good. For example, in the 50's and 60's the divorce rate among churchgoers was relatively lower than non-attenders nationwide. However today, many congregations have members who have experienced divorce while actively attending. So, what conclusions are we to draw from all this?

One, the church should not pretend to offer a perfect world. Allowing others to believe the church is perfect and that Christians are somehow perfect is the biggest lie we have even believed among ourselves. This myth along with the "one stop and shop" mentality, I believe has brought great harm to the institution itself.

Two, church stuff can be as simple as marketing the selling points of the church just like we would a business or another organization. When this happens, we are conveying the idea that what we have in here (the walls of the church) is better than what is out there. Sound familiar? Think about this. How many preachers craft sermons aimed at marketing the church while inadvertently developing a club mentality at the same time? Maybe the reason we come back without any miracle, God-intervening stories to tell is because our hands were full of selling points. Does this make sense?

2. The coming and going is only to build the body because the church believes it is the only magnet of the gospel.

Take another look at Figure 1. Ask this question. Where is God in this picture? Unfortunately, this picture illustrates how the opportunities to meet God are within the church. A closer look reveals most of us are unwilling to say or even admit. We have made the church as the magnet. Organizationally speaking, we have communicated that we are only powerful as the people of God when connected jointly to the church. In contrast, we are all magnets of the gospel and have access to the power of the Holy Spirit who resides within us. This missional concept will be teased out later in this chapter.

3. *To bring outsiders into a controllable formation which resembles the insiders of the church.*

This explains church competitiveness for more people to be counted, more buildings and more programs to offer more services (named as ministries). Not to mention, a bigger budget to sustain more ministries driven with the need to attract even more. Much is said about "doing" church and little is said about "being" the church. What's at stake? Control....Control.....Control.

Recognizing all the church stuff is the easy part. Church leaders see it. Church attenders and non-attenders see it. Even hard, hard-wired congregations, groups, denominations, see it. Everyone sees it. Right? So why can't we change?

Here's why.

The organizational realm of church reinforces our mechanical 20th Century thinking and programmed our mindset during the industrialized era. This hardwiring happened with the builder generation (our parents) and when the baby-boomers who now are the leaders of the church were just children. Simply said, boomers and builders have not considered another way of thinking or better yet, the importance of the relationship of the parts. Below is what most baby-boomers and builders see, trust and believe.

- In appearance, organization offers a network of people agreeing on core values, doctrine and practices.
- In appearance, organization makes things function better (mission statements, flow charts, calling trees, etc).
- In appearance, organization including job descriptions of staff and volunteers offers clearly marked areas of responsibility and accountability.
- In appearance, organization frames the structure.
- In appearance, organization has the appearance to solve all our problems.

The Relational Realm of Church

As followers of God in the everyday world, we are trying to reach our families, co-workers, and associates with the gospel while the church seeks to keep up and survive cultural insurgencies by reforming the religious institution. As a result, the church is missing the fundamental challenge of being the place where people will do their spiritual questing. Although she certainly has the right story and the right message for our culture, but the church is not creating venues for the message nor releasing her members to communicate the message in their favorite and most comfortable environments.

Entropy and Vacuums

In a culture that is receptive to the spiritual, the church today needs to be on point or on mission. It is as if a new kind of entropy or "church stuff" has settled into our church culture with blinding effects.

For example, making the call of "charging" or the "player-control foul," is the most controversial for basketball officials. The official must determine if the defensive player truly established position by filling a space on the basketball court. The defensive player must stand perfectly still long enough for the official to declare the space occupied and therefore render a foul on the offensive player with the ball charging into the defender. In almost every case, the defensive player, his teammates, his coach and especially the fans, all believed he had established position when the collision occurred. Likewise, the offensive player, his teammates, coach and fans all believe the defender did not fill the space in time. Depending on the call of the officials, a measure of disorder and displeasure follows for the player and team penalized for the infraction. Entropy is going from a state of order to a state of maximum disorder.

In a similar way, this new entropy and idolatrous self-delusion, embraced by church culture is largely due to a disagreement over the filling of space. The image of filling up space is especially compelling in Jesus' ministry and the mission he mandates to his followers.

Jesus created vacuums to fill in both nature and in people. Either wrong matter or spirit can fill the space. Often Jesus would enter in and fill the space with his presence and the people involved experienced freedom and redemption. Consider this.

In the Bible Jesus confronted bad teaching especially when a demoniac who was blind and mute was misrepresented by the religious leaders who declared him under the influence of Beelzebub, the ruler of demons. Instead, Jesus cast out their false theology and the demons with the Spirit of God. Then Jesus made this announcement. *"And if I drive out demons by Beelzebub, by whom do your people drive them out? So then, they will be your judges. But if I drive out demons by the Spirit of God, then the kingdom of God has come upon you" (Matthew 12:28-29 NIV).*

He further stated, *"When an evil spirit comes out of a man, it goes through arid places seeking rest and does not find it. Then it says, 'I will return to the house I left.' When it arrives, it finds the house unoccupied, swept clean and put in order. Then it goes and takes with it seven other spirits more wicked than itself, and they go in and live there. And the final condition of that man is worse than the first. That is how it will be with this wicked generation (Matthew 12:46 NIV).*

Simple creating a vacancy is not enough. Simply cleansing the situation is not enough either. The space itself is vulnerable to pressure from a fallen world that seeks to return, find the house "unoccupied, swept and put in order."

The presence of God must fill the space. By abdicating space, the latter becomes worse than the former state. Do you see the dilemma when the church fills this space with politics, programs and methods where the Spirit of God belongs? In other words, we take man-made matter to fill the God-spaced vacuums in our culture.

Moreover, Jesus makes a connection between personal filling and cultural filling. As Christians our mission and mandate is to fill both spaces. By doing so, this allows us to be "salt and light" in a secular society where Christians are witnessing and introducing today's culture to the Spirit.

As a church consultant, I have had the opportunity first hand to see how "church stuff" in churches and lack of clear missional leadership always leads to high control management. If you cannot lead and compellingly give a sense of direction, then control is all that is left. With high control management comes cultural captivity from within and from without because the forces at work are reactionary in nature.

Escaping church stuff necessitates that we embrace our failure to successfully disciple those who have come to the church. We filled the God-vacuum with other things. Then later wondered what happened. Our nation is not Christian just because there are no blue laws and lack of prayer in school. Instead, we have dropped the ball! Let us all face it, and then own it. Our efforts should be concentrated on releasing culturally captive church members from mundane "church stuff," by liberating them to participate in God's redemptive mission in their homes, schools, neighborhoods and communities.

The Missional Realm of Church

Well, here's the truth. It can often be much easier for individual followers of Jesus to escape all the church stuff than it is for churches and groups. Why? Because controlling resources and leading from position are not easily surrendered. The baggage is viewed as too great to give up. To do so, would require enormous trust cultivated by God in the heart. If that is the case, which I believe it is, then followers of Jesus need to find their freedom in real mission. As the people of God, we are to be linked to the church but the church should not be our focus. Seeing ourselves as the magnets of gospel is an admission that God is with me as I come and "as I go" into all the world.

Figure 2

Closely examine above Figure 2. Notice the coming and going that is already happening in North America today. This is consistent with the obvious interpretation that Jesus knew we would be on the go. So, the command is not to "go." Instead, there is only one command and that is to "make disciples of all nations."

Moreover, I have discovered that church members are better able and empowered to make disciples when they affirmed by church leadership to view their mission as their home, their school, their workplace, their neighborhood and etc. The mission is not the coming to the church itself.

Why? Because every follower of Christ is indeed a magnet of the gospel. We are the attraction to others. Not ourselves alone. It is the life (a special treasure within us) with our living through Christ, which becomes the attraction principle.

2 Corinthians 4: 7-11 RSV says, "But we have this treasure in earthen vessels, to show that the transcendent power belongs to

God and not to us. We are afflicted in every way, but not crushed; perplexed, but not driven to despair; persecuted, but not forsaken; struck down, but not destroyed; always carrying in the body the death of Jesus, so that the life of Jesus may also be manifested in our bodies. For while we live we are always being given up to death for Jesus' sake, so that the life of Jesus may be manifested in our mortal flesh."

To represent Christ trumps representing the institution or a particular affiliation.

Do you get it now? Let me say it in another way.

Incarnationally, the gospel is the intentional application of The Great Commission with active participation in the Kingdom of God where the vision of God (adopted by us), our missional behavior and our spirituality all **intersect** with the mission of God. The movie *World Trade Center* offers us a picture and a metaphor of what it means to face a 9/11 world in chaos where everything has collapsed and countless souls are trapped. The only thing we can do is to pray as we head into the mess like that lone Marine who climbed inside the rubble with a flashlight shouting, "tap or yell if you can hear me."

Fundamentally, our mission (both biblically formed and validated) defines our committed participation as God's people, at God's invitation and command, in God's own mission, within the history of God's world for the redemption of God's creation.

The Grand Narrative Is The True Story Of The World

The Bible clearly articulates God's vision, which tells a story, which is the story of all time for the entire world. It is the public truth about God's presence and meaning along with our destiny of universal history. It will take some un-learning of "church stuff" to fully approach the scriptures by seeing the mission God (with the participation of God's people), and to enthusiastically read the whole Bible by hearing what the text says with our own involvement in God's original mission.

Michael Goheen says that the horizon of God's mission as the ends of the earth is central to the biblical story from the beginning.

God's intention is to recover and restore all nations, all cultures and all peoples. God's purpose is absolutely comprehensive in nature and scope. His purpose involves more than a battle against sin and idolatry but a reclaiming of all creation to "place everything under his feet to glorify the Father" as mentioned in Ephesians chapter one. [2]

The missional invitation is inviting people to live within the story, not to live within the walls of the church. This means as people of God we are non-geographically based, multi-ethnic and sent to live in all cultures of the world. Of what do we have to be afraid? The gospel is translatable by its very nature and it affirms the grand purposes of God for redemption and judges the idolatrous deviations and twistings of God's mission often covered deep under the messy rubble of church stuff.

Having made known unto us the mystery of his will, according to his good pleasure, which he hath purposed in himself: that in the dispensation of the fulness of times he might gather together in one all things in Christ, both which are in heaven, and which are on earth; even in him. Ephesians 1:9-10 KJV

Interestingly, the story within the true story is our interpretation of scripture that revolves around the "sending" character of God and our participation in His long-term purpose.

Breathability And The Balance Of Unequals

Long ago in 1985 in Evansville, Indiana, I listened to John Killinger describe how denominations and churches were once movements. He talked about how church leaders gave organization to the movement in order to capture the fluidity. When this happened came structure and in some cases creeds, doctrine, and eventual dogma. In other words, organization provided the function for the movement so leaders would not feel powerless but in control of things. The downside. Organization can and usually does crystallize the movement and breatheability is choked.

Why? The relational and missional realities get lost in the mix if we aren't careful. So, to what should we pay attention?

The relational component of the mix contributes to the church's breatheability just as much as the missional does. This is what I am saying. Relationally within the movement, we embody the following characteristics:

- Interdependently dependent on God.
- Leaning on each other so we can lean on God.
- Networking together to build the Kingdom.
- Accomplishing as a group more than we can as individuals.
- Collaborating ministry and missional ideas in a breathing practice of inhaling and exhaling in cooperation with the Holy Spirit.

Moreover, trying to get a balance of organization, relational, and missional simply makes for an unhealthy church. Why is this true? Because they are not equal to begin with. This is where the rub comes in.

Distracted churches try to balance these unequal elements and find it easier to organize activity inside the church building, attract and involve more people in those activities. Then, they place the ministry label on it. Sound good? Now that you have read this far, I hope the previous statement sounds familiar but not good to you. My friend, there is much more to consider.

In the gospel, Jesus spent little time in the institutional church. He was not against it yet he regularly confronted the Pharisees and Sadducees. If anything, Jesus spent huge blocks of his time in relationship with his heavenly Father in spiritual and missional formation.

The spiritual formation of Jesus occurred to before every major decision he made such as the appointment of the Twelve or an encounter with a social outcast. He retreated to the mountains for prayer and soul development with the Father and it did not matter that others were searching for him.

"Thru Hiking" is Missional

In 1998, I hiked a section of the famous Appalachian Trail that runs through West Virginia. This is an example of a "section" hiker. Serious enthusiasts who complete the entire 2,175 miles of the AT from Georgia to Maine are called "thru hikers." Every spring 1,400 to more than 2,000 people set out to hike the entire. About one in four makes it. Researchers say 20 percent of the thru-hiker wannabes quit within the first 30 miles.

Completing a thru-hike entails numerous hurdles. Among them are blocking out the time (4-6 months) managing the expense, getting in shape, and developing the mental toughness. Many people think the journey is going to be something like an Indiana Jones adventure. But this is not the case. Instead, thru-hiking is a very subtle journey that builds as one goes along. You must decide how much mental, physical, emotional and spiritual energy you allot for each day. Each day, like each step of the journey, demands a certain stewardship of these energies so a deficit does not occur. After all, thru-hiking is not a race but a really, really long walk that requires pacing.

The missional formation of Jesus was the driven personality to carry out the mission of God. For instance, in John Chapter 4, he intentionally left Judea and went to Galilee. The scripture says, "He had to pass through Samaria"(verse 4). In other words, it was more than the route itself that led him to the City of Sychar to meet the Samaratian Woman at the well. Jesus hiked thru Samaria, the missional path where he would once again complete the vision of God.

About the Five Steps

The insights we have explored about the organizational, relational, and missional realms of the church point to a new way of improving the missional portions of church, and a platform on which to build the rest of the book. However, I doubt that just knowing these insights is going to turn anyone into a missional leader overnight. We need more explicitly, practical, and visible signposts to help us follow this new missional path. That is what the Five Steps to Transforming Distracted Churches provide.

The Five Steps evolved over years of conducting coaching workshops and listening to hundreds of people talk in public at Barnes & Noble, Staples, and restaurants. By listening to spiritual conversations over and over with so many different people, I was able to see lots of fascinating patterns in how people tried to coach each other when the church distraction was obvious. One pattern I noticed early on was that there were a limited number of possible directions to go in, which I have illustrated below in Figure 3 below.

Figure 3, Directions Spiritual Conversations Can Go

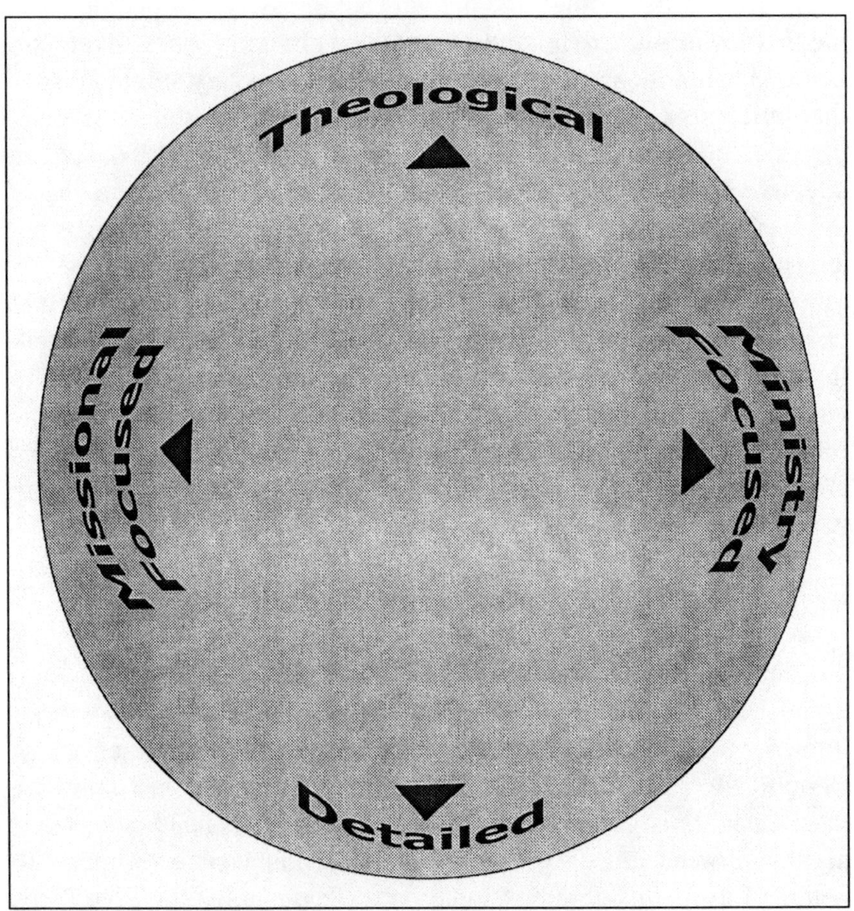

Spiritual conversations could go north and become too theological or south and get too detailed. It could go east and focus on the ministry or west and focus on the missional.

Unfortunately, when embarking on a spiritual conversation, one general direction always seems faster than all the others for accomplishing the goal. This general direction was to focus firmly on the ministry (every member a minister), without getting into the details. After identifying which direction was the fastest to focus on in the conversation, the next goal was to identify the path of least resistance and usually the shortest route from A to B. Point A being to get another person coming to the church, and point B to have the same person involved in the church's ministry. This is illustrated in Figure 4 below.

Figure 4, The Shortest Path from A to B

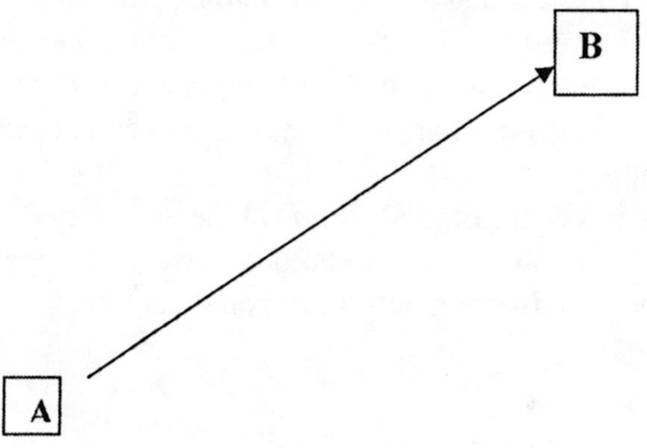

Taking the path of least resistance from Point A to Point B takes away from the individual with whom you are conversing, both the awareness and the opportunity to be missional. Therefore, because we have led them to the ministry aspect, they do not explore the missional any further. As leaders, we can steer the conversation, just as easily, toward the missional and accomplish greater results. This leads to fulfillment for the individual.

Over time and through watching hundreds of people explore different ideas, I gradually began to identify a missional path for efficient spiritual conversations. This missional path or process map had many different parts to it that all connected together, and the path itself was independent of the content of any dialogue. Over several years, I compiled and tested many different ways of communicating this missional path to others, keeping what worked and refining what did not. Eventually, this work emerged into a set of ideas I now call the Five Steps to Transforming Distracted Churches Who Leave Their *First* Love.

The Five Steps describe a new way for leaders to have spiritual conversations when they really want to help decision-makers of the church redirect their thinking away from the distraction and on to their *first* love. These steps describe a new way to interact, a new way to influence, a new way to stretch and grow people and a new way to join spiritual conversations.

The good news is that this new missional path intersects with the vision of God, provides purpose and creates completeness. The Five Steps describe the missional path of completeness when you want to help someone learn or change. Then, the church is changed by this new thinking.

Figure 5, is a visual representation of the Five Steps. This diagram may not make much sense just yet, but as we go through each step, you may find this diagram helpful to come back to.

Figure 5, The Five Steps to Transforming Distracted Churches

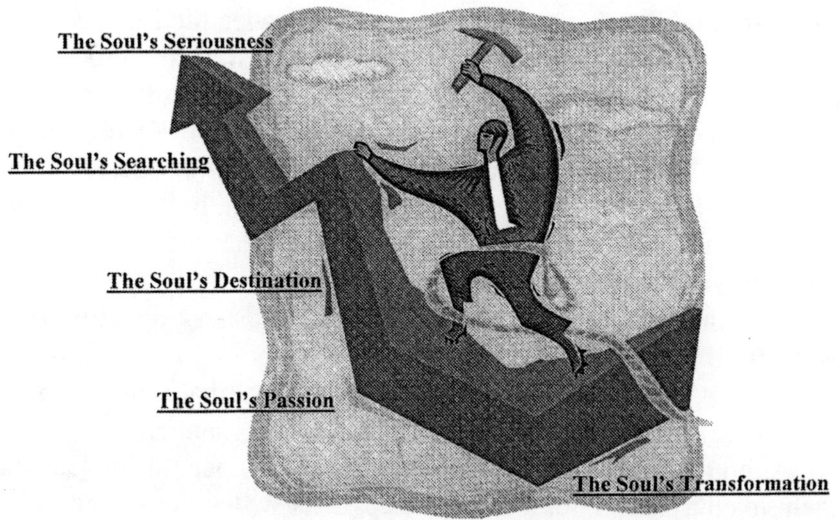

The first step to transforming distracted churches is learning about **The Soul's Transformation called Missional Spirituality.** This is the platform that every "thru hiker" must stand on. Much of the first step links directly with the desires, behaviors and habits of Jesus. We explore the concept of being empowered by the passion of Jesus, embracing Jesus' missionary purposes and how to engage culture to communicate the truth of Jesus.

The second step, **The Soul's Passion is called Missional Calling**. This is where spiritual leaders experience the compelling spirit of God to articulate current reality of the church and name the distraction. This is a by-product of a nourished soul shaped by the presence of Christ and faith formation in order to pursue missional change.

Step three is called **The Soul's Destination or Missional Visioning**. Here we work on improving our understanding and ability to recognize the presence of Christ in our faith movements.

This is critical as spiritual leaders for us to defining the missional quality of every word that comes out of our mouth.

The fourth step is called **The Soul's Searching or Missional Learning**. In this chapter, missional-driven leadership is introduced as a teaching model to help leaders understand the slow process of releasing church members to become missionaries to the community. The components of this model are Permission, Questioning, Guidance, Launching and Learning. It is based on Jesus' own coaching of his disciples before He sent them out, how they should behave while out on the missional path, and learning the value of renewal when they return back to Him.

The final step is called **The Soul's Seriousness or Missional Accountability**. Here we explore the transformation possibilities with a new kind of accountability or score sheet that reminds us of what to pay attention to when we see missional change.

Although I am explaining the Five Steps in a linear fashion, using them in churches is not a linear process. Each step does need to be mastered before you can achieve the best outcome of the following step. In other words, it is like building a house. Each construction phase is interesting on its own, but it is when all the steps come together that you really have something to inhabit.

In summary, the Five Steps are trail markers that point to a new path to follow when we advance the Kingdom of God by helping another person, or a church to change. The Five Steps show us a new way to lead, to evangelize, to be the church without comprising the message of the gospel.

Chapter Three

THE SOUL'S TRANSFORMATION: Missional Spirituality

"Many Christians sense that the focus, drive, and vision Jesus had—His sense of purpose in being—is supposed to be part of their experience too. Aren't we supposed to be centered and empowered in a clear vision of God's love and plan, as Christ was? Yet somehow we find ourselves more often wandering at the margins—keeping one eye on God and another scouting the landscape for a more exciting offer. We drift into halfheartedness and boredom, losing our passionate center."

—Howard Baker

Introduction

Watching the Discovery Channel is a favorite pastime of mine. The February 18, 2007 episode about Raptors captivated my interest. Raptors, birds such as hawks and falcons, are among nature's most extreme aerialists. Raptors and other birds use two common techniques known as thermal soaring and dynamic soaring. Since most of their time is utilized expending energy searching for food on the fly, they each learn to perfect the art of soaring early on.

They take advantage of the natural atmosphere and the benefits of updraft. For example, studies of these aerial creatures show that air currents often rise up the side of a mountain, tall buildings and even trees create updrafts so birds can ride for extra altitude.

Thermal soaring, in particular, happens when the sun hearts the earth and air above it. The warmer layer of air near the surface and the difference in temperature between warm air and the surrounding air starts to rise. Birds, sail planes, and gliders, can take advantage of this rising vortex of air and essentially climb several hundred meters without expending any energy. The only risk involved is to fly in a "free fall" descent toward the ground and allow the rising air to generate a spectacular lift. When this occurs, the birds never flap their wings. Instead, they can go for miles just bouncing back and forth on these powerful wind gusts, pulling up a little bit each time they are hit by one.

Isn't that amazing? Of more amazement is the opportunity the North American church has to take advantage of the natural atmosphere where this culture has a genuine God-interest and God is at work in the culture and in individual lives. Does this sound interesting to you? It should.

There is more to consider. As the people of God we also have the opportunity to "soar on the updraft" or the passion of Jesus.

There is a great deal of essential concepts to absorb in this chapter. Read it thoroughly and relate the material to real-life situations as often as possible. You have explored the book's explanation of *first* love, distracted churches, and the basic thesis of "every member a missionary."

This chapter will teach you about missional spirituality. As you read this section, focus on what distracted churches offer to their members and compare them in terms of advantages and disadvantages. As you are studying the material, ask yourself these questions. "What does the church have that the world cannot live without?" "What do you have that the world cannot live without?"

In general, this section will help build a foundation for the Five Steps that will make it easier for you to learn the rest of the material in this book, so it is important for you to master these ideas before moving on to the next chapter. Turn back a few pages and look at Figure 5 again. The Soul's Transformation is the foundational step for all the other steps to follow along the missional path. This section has as much importance as the foundation does for the construction of a house. If there are cracks in the foundation, changing the music, or style of worship will not fix it.

This chapter details missional spirituality as your soul's transformation that will directly affect you as a disciple.

Listed below in order are the ingredients of missional spirituality.

- Aligned ***with*** and empowered ***by*** the passion of Jesus.
- Embrace Jesus' missionary purposes
- Engage culture to communicate the truth of Jesus

The first section defines missional spirituality as being aligned with and empowered by the passion of Jesus (His desires, His behavior and His passionate center).

Next, you will be challenged to embrace Jesus' missionary purposes. Finally, you will be asked to courageously engage today's culture so you can communicate the truth of Jesus.

Aligned With and Empowered By the Passion of Jesus

Let's look, first of all, at the way spiritual conversation came about between Jesus and His father.

"For I have come down from heaven, not to do my own will, but the will of him who sent me; and this is the will of him who sent me, that I should lose nothing of all that he has given me, but raise it up at the last day For this is the will of my Father, that every one who sees the Son and believes in him should have eternal life; and I will raise him up at the last day." John 6:37-40 RSV

These verses tell us that God gave Jesus human capital and that He should lose no one. As a result, Jesus saw every conversation as a spiritual conversation. He made immediate associations to the call of God on people's lives—the pull of God on the hearts of men. This was not cleverness or spiritualizing the conversations on his part. So, why did Jesus see every conversation as a spiritual conversation?

The Desire of Jesus

The desire of His heart is for the heart of every man. Think about this. When your heart is for the heart of every man, your heart cannot be for yourself or for the church. It has to be for the Kingdom. This was the desire of Jesus!

For example, underlying the story of Jesus' encounter with the Woman at the Well mentioned in John 4 is His desire. *"Every one who drinks of this water will thirst again, but whoever drinks of the water that I shall give him will never thirst; the water that I shall give him will become in him a spring of water welling up to eternal life" (John 4:13-14 RSV).*

God has given every disciple human capital as well. These people live in our homes, schools, neighborhoods and workplaces and they are our responsibility. Do you believe God has placed you where you are as your mission? I do.

The Passionate Center

Spiritual leaders will not follow another spiritual leader who says, "We are going to reach the lost or invite someone to come to church next week." These admonishments have become dull.

It is not monumental for followers to follow leaders. But it is monumental when leaders follow a leader because that leader has a passionate center for what he or she is doing. This is why the twelve disciples followed Jesus. They were leaders who saw the passionate center of Jesus. Unlike the crowds, they did not follow Him for miracles or bread provisions. They were anticipating a new kingdom that Jesus was passionate about but they did not understand how the Kingdom of God was about the kingly reign in men's hearts instead of a political and military rule.

So, go ahead and speak up. It is good for the soul. It is what moves us. After our passionate center of is recognized by those we influence, then comes the inspiration. The inspiration is what is missing in many people who want to desperately effect spiritual change.

When we create a passionate center corresponding to the passion of Jesus, we feel motivated to do something, which changes our face and voice. When you watch for it, you can see that the act of creating a passionate center is a specific event. It is possible to pinpoint the exact moment it occurs. This is the moment of breakthrough, a moment when we see an answer to a challenge.

When people are inspired, they see how it is bringing the Kingdom of God to bear. Bringing the Kingdom of God to bear will mean having a very different set of ministries that leave behind the institutional church.

Church planting and multiple-site churches bring the Kingdom of God to bear in a fresh new way. People are deployed into a community to become part of that community and not just to start another house of worship. They may indeed attract potential believers but the primary focus of the core group(s) is to exercise their passionate center as it reflects the passion of Jesus.

How does "bringing the Kingdom of God" to bear look like among passionate Christians who are passionate centered?

- A person living in the Kingdom of God…Finds their identity in Christ
  Read Colossians 2:6-12

We find our value and worth more and more in the reality of who we are in Christ.

We live grounded in the truth of who we are to Him, and we are less attached to and influenced by false programs for happiness. Thus, we grow in humility as we understand who we are.

- A person living in the Kingdom of God…Abiding with Christ when abiding isn't easy
  Read 1 John 2:18-28

We are not gritting our teeth trying to do what Jesus says. Rather, we are growing in our desire to do what Jesus says. As we abide in Him and He abides in us, we experience freedom and begin to taste the life Jesus came to give us.

When we first become Christian, the pursuit of spiritual life feels easy. There is a natural desire to know more about God. You are hungry to read the Bible, your heart fills up with joy in worship and the things that once tempted you seem to lose their grip on you. Your heart is tender toward God and toward people.

But for most of us, something happens. It may be sudden or it may be gradual. What once was real, simple, and enjoyable has now become an effort and difficult. We may find it hard to sense God presence, and the Bible may become dull to us.

The spiritual dryness or dullness could be the direct result of a deliberate sin that need to be confessed on our part. Or, it happens as a rhythm in our spirituality. You may ask, "Why does God allow it? Why can't it always feel the way it felt at first?"

Closer examination of this reveals how energy looks different in times of joy and in times of sorrow. In other words, different seasons of the spiritual life call for different practices. Abiding is not one single practice. We must adjust to our season of life.

- A person living in the Kingdom of God…Manifests the fruit of the Spirit
  Read Galatians 5:22-26

As we become God's temple, what we take into our selves through our thoughts, eyes, ears and mouth gradually change. The process is attractive and redemptive to us and to those around us.

- A person living in the Kingdom of God…cares for the outcast
  Read Matthew 25:34-40

What breaks God's heart, begins to break ours. We see people who are often rejected by the world, through Jesus' eyes. As we grow in humility, we see ourselves in the outcast and we realize we are more like the outcasts than not.

Consider this song taken from the soundtrack to "The Hunchback of Notre Dame."

God Help the Outcasts

Don't know if You can hear me,
or if You're even there.
I don't know if You will listen
to a humble prayer.

They tell me I am just an outcast.
I shouldn't speak to You.
Still, I see Your face and wonder,
were You once an outcast, too?

God help the outcasts,
hungry from birth
Show them the mercy
they don't find on Earth.
The lost and forgotten,
they look to You still.
God help the outcasts,
or nobody will.

I ask for nothing,
I can get by,
but I know so many
less lucky than I.
God help the outcasts,
the poor and downtrod.
I thought we all were
the children of God.

I don't know if there's a reason
why some are blessed, some not.
Why the few You seem to favor,
they fear us, flee us,
try not to see us.

I don't know if there's a reason
why some are blessed, some not.
Why the few You seem to favor,
they fear us, flee us,
try not to see us.

God help the outcasts,
the tattered, the torn.
Seeking an answer to why they were born.
Winds of misfortune
have blown them about.
You made the outcasts,
don't cast them out.
The poor and unlucky,
the weak and the odd.
I thought we all were
the children of God. [2]

- A person living in the Kingdom of God…experiences the depth of God's love
  Read 1John 2:28

How do you act when you are not at the top of your game and when you come to God and you have not prayed well or at all? If you are like me, you have probably felt like a hindrance. I know I have. But then I realize my brokenness give Christ the opportunity to say again, "I love you and you are on my team."

You may ask, "What can I do?" Here are a few suggestions.

1. Listen to and join spiritual conversations
2. Focus on spending time each week with people who don't go to church
3. Humbly take the spiritual pulse of your church and be prepared to offer missional solutions.

The Behavior of Jesus

Beginning at the age of twelve, Jesus listened intently to the stories of the doctors and lawyers. When he launched his public ministry, he listened to the stories of ordinary folks. He already knew their story but he knew they needed to tell it. This behavior allowed him to exercise his coaching of lives with transforming power.

So much of what we do in the church is to inform thru bible study, leadership training, and church activities. But the behavior of Jesus was to transform.

Shouldn't our purpose be to be a conduit of the same transforming power of Jesus? Has the church forgotten its transforming purpose? Does the church exist as a "how-to" conduit?

In our day, for some reason, many do not know how to confess sin in a way that coaches life, growth and change. Spiritually wise people always knew how to do it but unfortunately, Protestant churches in particular, have failed to provide a structure beyond the capacity to judge sinner. Jesus provided a structure for forgiveness that provided a way to grow out of your sin. This is a kind of indispensable life-coaching tool and is desperately needed today.

Together we can learn and practice a confession that allows us to experience God's forgiveness and coaching others to look at the past, let go of it, not be defeated by it, and grow toward Christlikeness.

The problem is not a lack of information. We have heard plenty of sermons about grace. Plus, many Christians may experience a moment of grace but not a lifetime of grace. For instance, let's say a highway patrolman pulls you over for speeding. He follows up with a warning and some coaching. The warning provides a moment of grace experience but the coaching enables living by grace.

Dietrich Bonhoeffer said,

> "Confess your faults one to another' (Jas. 5:16). He who is alone with his sin is utterly alone. It maybe with Christians not withstanding corporate worship with all their common prayers, fellowship and service may still be left with all their aloneness.

The final breakthrough to fellowship does not occur because they have fellowship with one another as believers and devout people. They do not have fellowship as sinners. The pious fellowship permits no one to be a sinner. So everyone must conceal his sin from himself and others, and from the fellowship.

We dare not be sinners. Many Christians are unthinkably horrified when a real sinner is suddenly discovered among the righteous. So, we remain alone with our sin, living in lies and hypocrisy. The fact is we are sinners." [1]

So, what is the bottom line behavior? God does not need confession to give it but we need it in order to heal and change. Confession and the life coaching that follows is not an accounting procedure. Confession is a tool for personal growth and missional development.

So let us stop for a moment and reflect on the ideas I have put forward so far, and see what they might add up to.

1. Missional spirituality happens when people align themselves with and are empowered by the passion of Jesus and create a passionate center for the Kingdom of God inspiring to others;
2. Missional spirituality happens when people provide a structure for confession and life coaching as tools for personal growth and missional development.

It becomes clear why our job as leaders should be to help people make their own connections to the missional path. This is a new way of thinking and a new world to explore here. These are some of the most important skills that leaders must master today, and central to transforming distracted churches who leave their first love.

Embrace Jesus' Missionary Purposes

Luke Chapter 15 pulls back the curtain for us to embrace Jesus' missionary purposes. During this time in His ministry, Jesus attracted criticism from church leaders and curiosity from sinners due to his talk of the Kingdom of God.

"Now the tax collectors and sinners were all drawing near to hear him. And the Pharisees and the scribes murmured, saying, 'This man receives sinners and eats with them." Luke 15:1-2 RSV

Jesus responded by initiating a conversation composed of parables or stories about the missing sheep, the missing coin, and the missing son. After all, most everyone has experienced missing something due to the misled, the misplaced, and the misguided.

Luke 15 is about finding the missing. It is not about finding the obvious but finding the less obvious. They are missing because of our obscurity intentions. So much of our effort in church is to rewrite Luke 15 and focus on the condition of the lost item or person.

Unfortunately, we spend too much time talking about this lost condition of people and not enough time finding the missing. The motive for telling these stories in the first place is not to focus on the missing but to zero in on how they were sought and found.

This is precisely what distracted churches do.

Churches and individuals who embrace Jesus' missionary purposes discuss among themselves and their assistants how they will respond through celebration when the missing are indeed found. For example, good parents know that celebrating how tall our children have grown or how many pounds our children have gained is nothing compared to the celebration of that child's birthday. Why? Because we are celebrating who they are!

This is exactly what Jesus did. His missionary purpose was to celebrate the importance of every person He came in close proximity. When I first started studying the Bible, I was taught that Jesus' ministry was within a limited 200-mile radius. For years, I focus on how it appeared that He was limited compared to modern travel today. Then, I made a new discovery. Jesus' missional efforts led Him to encounters that too many were simply "out of range" or "off the map." Nevertheless, Jesus never passed by the uniqueness of every spiritual conversation regardless of the condition or the practices and living standards of the sinner.

Consider that not all of Jesus missional encounters were recorded in scripture. In fact, scripture tells us so. But we should be thankful that many of them are. So how should we view those encounters?

We need to see with Kingdom lenses. Otherwise, we may resign ourselves that missional impact is not measurable in quantitative terms and retreat to old and familiar patterns of church growth. This is difficult for distracted churches who attempt being missional without immediate results.

However, there is the importance of being celebrative when measurable standards cannot be applied to the missional activity we did. Consequently, we do not celebrate enough in church. So let me challenge you to think of some creative ways your church can celebrate when the missing are found. Maybe this is reason why many do not return to church. Could it be that when they do return, they see that the rest of us have quickly moved on to the next program on our agenda and neglected to rejoice over what has been accomplished? Think how you would feel if this happened to you.

Engage Culture to Communicate the Truth of Jesus

Obviously, attracting people to the church is not necessarily wrong. In fact, missional spirituality has an attractional aspect to it as a continuation of the previously discussed concepts of creating a passionate center that inspires others.

Leith Anderson, pastor of Wooddale Church near Minneapolis says, "I think attractional is really a subset of missional. Churches ought to be attractional. After all, there is an attractive appeal to the mission. Churches that don't attract people to the gospel or even to the institution will not live out the mission because they won't live at all. The problem arises when attracting people to the church becomes the mission."[3]

Consider how desolate and used culture becomes when attracting people to our church is our mission. If we are not careful, our churches can easily stereotype subsets and homogeneous groups of people to attract because up front we identified them as useful to pay for our ministries, our budgets, and our buildings.

For instance, I hear church leaders tout the number of mission trips they plan each year for both youth groups and adult groups to go to Mexico with a price tag of $2400 each. Many of these churches, not all of them, would never consider reaching out to Hispanic or the inner-cities of the poor and the neglected even within driving distance of the church. Why? Because going on a mission trip to another country is glamorous. If the truth were known, many of these planned trips are to generate funds for some denominational mission department. Often the church announcements are not for skilled workers who have expertise. Those mission executives who are budget conscious ask for anyone to go and catch the wave of excitement. In fact, many of the groups come back to their home churches to report on how much fun they had. To others, it means recognition.

Why do I mention this? Consider how a local church could be missional within their community and take the $2400 of 10 people and use it for outreach to safe houses, food pantries, school supplies for children, fund summer jobs for troubled kids, pay Christian camp fees for low income children, and disperse funds to city parks and recreational areas to use for neighborhood improvements.

Before we dive into another transforming step, let's explore further this last major piece of missional spirituality. Engaging culture to communicate the truth of Jesus consists of four linear, sequential action steps.

Action Step One: Outwardly focused on a world waiting to know God
Action Step Two: Celebrate people for who they are
Action Step Three: Encouraging the fleshing out of what people believe is God's mission for the world
Action Step Four: Cast a wide net for ideas for transforming the community

Outwardly Focused On a World Waiting To Know God

The teachers of the church growth movement made us aware that the longer we are Christians and in the church, the fewer friends we have in the world. Interestingly, they offered no solutions for us to stay connected with worldly people because a fundamental ideology of separating ourselves underpins much of our religious thought and practice.

When we separate ourselves, two things are at work. (1) We view non-Christians and unchurched as toxic and (2) they are beyond redemption. Often our judgment is evident in our mannerisms, in our words, and our facial expressions.

This was not true of Jesus. He was condemned by the Pharisees and the Sadducees for eating and consorting with sinners. He selected the Twelve from among the ranks of tax collectors, fishermen, pro-Roman government and anti-Roman government extremists.

Today, the North American church has a wonderful opportunity to engage a culture that wants to know God. God interest can be seen everywhere. It is on billboards, media, movies, advertisements politics, and the marketing strategies of many successful companies. Is the church afraid to join the spirituality talk in the break rooms of law firms, at the water cooler, and the school teachers' lounge? I believe some are. Some of the strategy talks we have in the church to reach people begin by teaching one another how to argue scripture, prove your point, and defend the existence of God. What a waste of time.

Our changing times have yielded outrageous opportunities for the church to go beyond the place where most of church expression has conventionally happened. People are itching to be the church in some of the most unlikely places but where their friends visit.

For example, I know of one tanning salon owner who leads a bible study in her salon every week in a nearby town. Non-Christian clients are encouraged to participate in non-confrontive and non-threatening ways. The owner believes she is being the church to those who would not visit a church on Sunday.

Spirituality is in. When I worked at Staples Office Superstore in Cape Girardeau, I heard more spiritual talk than I heard in the walls of the church. Many of my fellow associates were college age youth who would openly discuss their hunger for the holy and God's intervention in their lives.

For instance, one associate named John told me everyday during the 18 months I work as a sales associate, how God worked in his life. When he talked about God's power in his life, it was certainly contagious and refreshing. It is something I rarely see in the church because church people want to discuss the weather or church stuff.

Celebrate People for Who They Are

Do people know that you are genuinely interested in them? If so, how do you show it?

First of all, we can show our genuine interest in them as individuals whether they are redeemed by God or not because they are made in His image with His grace upon their lives and with the capacity to godliness.

Second, we can show our genuine interest in them as individuals by being with them when they are being ungodly in their manners, actions, and talk. This takes a lot of courage for Christians but it sends a strong signal of association to the sinner. We can still be around them and still not approve of their behavior. As long as they know we do not disapprove of them as a friend, co-worker, or associate, then we have future opportunities to influence.

Third, I have always believed it was healthy in relationships with ungodly people to talk about my own imperfections and failures. That way I become a different model of Christian who does not feel superior or better in any way. Moreover, this demonstrates how the transforming power of God has shaped me and given me ownership and forgiveness of my failure.

Encourage the Fleshing Out Of What People Believe is God's Mission for the World

I am sure by now you have figured out there is a sequential order to be followed in engaging culture. Each of the four steps becomes more challenging and requires more courage than the previous step. This one is no exception.

Let me begin by saying that the church is cocooned with layers of history, polity, doctrine, dogma, and values. This is a strength not a weakness. However, what is often our strength becomes our weakness. In this case, the church is often incapable of talking about what it means to be the church.

Writing mission and purpose statements in the 80's was a positive step in the right direction, but they lacked clear actions and accountability. In fact, many churches print their mission statement each week on their bulletin, their newsletter, and their website. Yet, if you were to ask church attenders how the mission was being accomplished no one, and in some cases the pastor, could provide a satisfactory answer.

Focus groups where unchurched people are invited to talk would be useful. Focus groups, with the feedback of the unchurched, would give the church action steps that can go with the mission statements we have not used for years.

Let us be really honest. The church is so "fogged in" that we have great difficulty articulating what it means to be the church. Many churches think they are being missional by giving financial support to missions when in fact there are people all around them who do not receive any relational contact whatsoever from church members.

Cast a Wide Net for Ideas for Transforming the Community

Here again, is an opportunity for the church to receive outside input. Sometimes our ideas for serving the community come with strings attached. I can remember when churches scheduled a special Sunday to honor government leaders. So, they would invite the mayor, the chief of police, council members, and other dignitaries. But the underlying motive of the church was to get up a big crowd and to attract visitors. Even if they came from another church, the goal was met.

Recent mission trips by church groups to assist Katrina victims provided the much-needed volunteer assistance in immediate recovery. Disaster relief teams provided not only the manpower but also the spiritual encouragement folks needed. Upon return, most groups reported about the fulfillment they received in helping their neighbors. This is the kind of thing I am talking about.

Church leaders should regularly brainstorm together, with the input from outsiders, innovative and creative ways to transform their communities, cities, and neighborhoods.

At the beginning of this chapter, I urged you to ask yourself two questions. "What does the church have that the world cannot live without" "What do you have that the world cannot live without?"

Think about this. The world can live without our music, our programs, our ministries and even much more. But the one thing the church has and each individual Christian possesses is the transforming power of God. Do you want your children, your grandchildren, your friends, your work associates, future generations to live without the transforming power of God? If you agree with me, then fan the flames of missional spirituality.

Chapter Four

THE SOUL'S PASSION: Missional Calling

To become a spiritual adventurer means learning to listen for the voice of God. This listening involves a certain level of risk and vulnerability that does not come easily...[But] we cannot fully rest until we find our way back to the place of our soul's origin, back to the Love that gives us life.

–Marjorie J. Thompson

Introduction

We have now completed the first step toward transforming distracted churches who leave their first love. We know that missional spirituality is not about what Christians believe or what Christians do. It is easy to talk about a moral code appropriate for followers of Jesus. After all, the commandments and moral codes are formulated in mission statements and mission strategies.

Eugene Peterson said,

"The great weakness of North American spirituality is that it is all about us: fulfilling our potential, getting in on the blessings of God, expanding our influence, finding our gifts, getting a handle on principles by which we can get an edge over the competition. And the more there is of us, the less there is of God." [1]

In Step Two, we explore the soul's passion or missional calling. This concept is particularly relevant in our communication-saturated world. In this chapter, we will explore how the missional calling shapes us not just once at conversion but continuously and slowly.

Some Christians are like kayakers on a swift flowing river with patches of whitewater. There is never a doubt where they are going. They are going where the course of the river takes them.

Christians who desire to have their soul shaped by the calling of God on their life proceed at a different pace. Their soul's progression is like a canoe on a quiet lake, drifting and leisurely going along so they can take in the vistas of the shoreline, noticing rock formations, observing a blue heron fishing in the weeds, and enjoying the sun's reflection in the glassy water.

The church itself cannot be your still water. So, I am not advocating a call for a "deeper life" with another bible study or another ministry activity. Instead, I am asking you to intentionally turn off your cell phone, put away your palm pilot for a time and pay attention to the Spirit. The calling in cooperation with the Holy Spirit will be doing in you what Jesus did among his followers.

The Calling Continuously Shapes or Forms the Soul

The missional calling continuously shapes the individual so the mission remains the mission. Notice how Jesus prepared his disciples for his departure. Fifteen times in scripture, Jesus tells them he is leaving and twenty-six times, he tells them that he and his Father are sending the Holy Spirit.

This calling shapes the soul in a validating sort of way. Their mission became the process where Christ and the Holy Spirit focused their heart, their passion, and their experiences in a direction which clearly intersected with the mission of God. This points to the importance that they saw themselves as missionaries before others did. They proclaimed kingdom living guided by His "leaving and sending" just as much or maybe more so because Jesus was still with them. In no way was his departure or Christ's part a walking out or abandonment.

Leaving and Sending > Saying and Doing = Being (Identity)

Jesus' departure translated "leaving and sending" for the disciples so their mission would be about saying and doing. What Jesus did among them was continued in the disciples as they went saying and doing in their known world. This includes us as well.

Look at these scriptures in John's gospel.

I washed your feet; you wash one another's feet. (13:14)
I have loved you; you love one another. (13:34;15:12)
You have seen me; you will do my work. (14:9)
You have seen me work; you will do my work. (14:12)
I have been with you; the Spirit will be with you. (14:16-17)
I live; you also will live. (14:19)
You are in me; I am in you. (14:20)
I am teaching you; the Spirit will teach/remind you. (14:25-26)
Abide in me; I abide in you. (15:4)
I was hated; you will be hated. (15:26-27)
The Spirit will testify; you will testify. (15:26-27)
I go away; the Spirit will come. (16:7)
I have not finished what I have to say; the Spirit will tell you. (16:12-15).

Saying and Doing

Saying and doing practices the presence of Christ. Just like the "leaving and sending" shaped the disciples souls, the saying and doing has the same effect. Saying and doing work together like inhaling and exhaling. There is a special rhythm of back and forth illustrated by the scripture verses in Chapters 13, 14, 15, and 16 in John's gospel. The best and most powerful thing about it all is the presence of Christ who journeys with us on this missional path.

Missional calling is much bigger than a church "on mission" or "doing mission work." George Hunsberger stated it this way:

> "Mission is not something the church does, a part of its total program. No, the church's essence is missional, for the

calling and sending action of God forms its identity. Mission is founded on the mission of God in the world, rather than the church's effort to extend itself." [2]

Being or Identity

Missional calling is to participate **with** God in what He is doing and **in** His mission of redemption. With and in are powerful, connecting, relation-forming words. Peterson calls it "prepositional-participation." [3] In this dynamic, we never become the subject or the predicate. We are not the subject of the Christian life, nor do we perform the action of the Christian life.

Let me say it another way. I have heard too many sermons and discussions where a speaker or leader stands up in front of people and asks, "How can I know God's will for my life?" The question sounds noble and syrupy; dripping like honey off-the tongue," of someone who is trying to appear as a purpose-driven Christian. However, this is the wrong question because it is about you and me and not about God and His mission. It becomes a copout we conveniently use as distracted individuals and distracted churches.

Instead, we are invited or commanded into the ways and means of being in on, of participating in, what God is up to. We cannot participate with God and demand that we have our way. Sounds simple, but most of us think we have to tell God how we think things should be done. The ways and means must be appropriate to the ends they serve.

Knowing this, we become equipped and empowered to name the distraction not only in our personal life but in our church as well. Have you identified your distraction? Have you identified the distraction you see in your church?

It is no surprise we often return from our ministry sprints dodging sin, like one who leans their body forward, covers their head with a newspaper or book hoping to keep themselves from getting wet during a rainstorm. Come on. Let's get real. The leading reason church leaders come back "empty-handed" with no new enrollees for church is because our hands were full of selling points and not stained with the missional colors of God mission. Could this be the source of your frustration and distraction?

"For we are the aroma of Christ to God among those who are being saved and among those who are perishing, to one a fragrance from death to death, to the other a fragrance from life to life. Who is sufficient for these things? For we are not, like so many, peddlers of God's word; but as men of sincerity, as commissioned by God, in the sight of God we speak in Christ" (2 Corinthians 2:15-17 RSV).

Interview

On a rainy June morning at a local coffee shop, the author interviewed a public school teacher for this book. This teacher shared his passion for his work and his missional view of his career path.

Russell Grammer is a 4th grade teacher at Jefferson Elementary. He teaches all subjects except Missouri History and Social Studies. He is a Christian who attends a non-denominational church.

BARRY: *How do you view teaching at Jefferson Elementary as your mission?*

RUSSELL: *I think it was really a calling.*

BARRY: *Talk about that*

RUSSELL: *I believe it was from God absolutely. God has a sense of humor in that He has connected me in the exact line of work that I couldn't stand. And I heard the calling. To me the job of teaching is all about relationships, all about our kids, connecting with them, communicating with them—as opposed to giving them academic information.*

So in essence, when I get up in the morning, I'm already thinking about my students, the difficult ones who tend to give you heartaches. I pray for them and ask God to give me insight to break through the walls and connect with them.

BARRY: *Obviously, in public education, there are boundaries, parameters concerning discussions about God. Being a Christian yourself, when those God moments come and there's God interest, how do you handle that? What happens inside you?*

RUSSELL: *That's a very deep question and I struggle with that so many times because many times I'm looking at my students and I'm thinking the one thing that will really make all the difference in their whole life I am restricted on. I am not allowed to share. And that's really difficult and then on the other side I would not want my own children ever to be indoctrinated according to a certain person's views. And so I also understand the freedom and I respect that. But you said the God-moments, when they come up. It is so clear to me and it so obvious that this is the golden nugget of the school year. This is what God intended to happen. And it is always something that is never arranged, it is never planned. It's like a student says something and another students will often share their bit or their piece. And the next thing I know, I'm saying, "Oh, I'm watching God at work right here." A couple of examples. I remember one day, one of the most difficult students I ever had. He was only in my class for science. But we had just switched classes and he was on his way back to his classroom and he said, "Mr. Grammer" He called me into this little hallway section and he said, "I just got baptized." And the moment he said that, he knew that was important to me. He sensed it. That moment he said that I almost cried because that is the most wonderful thing. You are making a devotion with your whole life. That will make everything for you better— the best that it can be, if you'll live it.*

Another student, this year, he would just sometimes ask me questions and the students know what I believe. I don't keep my beliefs hidden from the students. And maybe some people would view that as wrong. I don't know. I sometimes wonder about that, but I always preface everything I say to the students with, "This is the way I see things. Not everybody does. A lot of people would completely disagree with me." And then I might say something, "I can't help. It's who I am. I can't really hide that." But this one student would ask me questions about scripture like, "What does it mean to deny yourself? How do you do that?" And that's a really deep question. And for a 4th grade boy to ask me that and really to be thinking about it and searching for an answer. And then the next day or the next week, he came back and he said, "I think I've figured it out." I could tell he had been really pondering it. He told me what he thought it means to "deny himself" like putting other people first and stuff like that. Sometimes those God moments, there's not even a word about God spoken—not at all.

A 2nd grade boy came into my room this year. The teacher didn't know what to do with him. She needed help with discipline. She came and dropped him off. And it was kind of like this. When she came to me, she said, "I had to take him to Mr. Cook, but I was praying that he wouldn't be there because I just had that feeling that he needed to talk to you." And it just happened that Mr. Cook had left the building just a minute before that. So her prayer was answer in that. So she brought the boy down to me and sometimes I get really stern. And I intimidate, scare into submission of authority. That's a healthy thing. I couldn't take that approach with this boy. I was looking at him and then I was praying the whole time, "God what do you have for this boy? What's going on with him?" He was in 2nd grade, right—anger issues. He was like gripped up; teeth clinched—wouldn't hardly look at me. And all of the sudden, it just came out of my mouth, "You know, when you grow up, you're gonna be a good father to your children. And you're gonna be a good husband because you'll love your wife like crazy. And you're gonna take care of your family. You're gonna be such a good parent and such a good husband." And that's not the kind of thing I would normally think about saying to a 2nd grade boy. But it was just there. The moment those words came out of my mouth, tears popped out of this boy's eyes. And he looked at me and it was like he was looking at me thinking, "I so much want to believe this." It was like everything in his life had told him contrary to that. And that was a God-moment even though there was nothing spoken about God.

BARRY: *Let's talk about God's redemptive purposes. I think you and I would agree that we receive salvation as Christians, but there's more than that. It's not so we go to heaven and that's it. We have the opportunity to participate in God's redemptive purpose for the world. Talk about the part you play, how you see your life playing, being a part of God's redemptive purposes.*

RUSSELL: *I think that's a fascinating question. There's a scripture that comes to mind about, "We are the fragrance of Christ." I know that it's more like people are reading my life and they are seeing God live through somebody. And I have the idea that God uses me much more often and much more powerfully when I'm totally unaware of it—than the times that I think, "God is really using me right now." So I think the redemptive purpose in my life simply comes down to me being the open vessel, a good steward of what He's given. So I understand, in my mind and heart, that everything I own and everything I am is at His complete disposal. He does whatever he wants to with it. And to me it's a position that I take before Him. He's my father. He knows what's best for me. I trust Him in that and therefore, everything is His. I don't try to hold anything back from Him.*

BARRY: *How important is life-coaching today?*

RUSSELL: *To me it's another word for discipleship or mentoring. We use a lot of phrases with that. I think it's as important today as it's ever been. But more so because we have such, I hate the broken family situation in our country. That terrifies me because when our families are broken there's no strength of unity, there's no foundational group of people. We're basically open society to whatever wants to come along and lead us—rule us. It's very frightening. And so I think it's important in that respect, but I'm sad to see that there are probably many believers who have more of an approach to life of "How will I be affirmed by my brothers and sisters in Christ" rather than looking around, listening attentively to what their Father is saying, God, about "How does that person right there need love? How does that one need love?" You know when you love that person, you are loving me—God saying that. That is the discipleship or life coaching that has to happen—like there is no more perfect connection we can make. Jesus said, That they will be one with me as I am also one with you. He was always attentive to what His Father was doing. I must be about my Father's business. If we are like that, He actually intends for our lives to look like His. It blows my mind that there can be a person walking by on the street right there—God already knows all his issues. God speaks something through me—drops the exact right word that that guys been mulling over for years. He drops it in there. That guy understands something or makes a connection that he has been desperately looking for. I mean, to me we serve the one who sets up those life skills or life training.*

BARRY: *Let me ask you about this. There are spiritual conversations that come up in the teacher's lounge, maybe in the hallways, things like that. Talk about that if you would. Are you very sensitive to those spiritual conversations? I know you are. Do you see it as an opportunity? Does it come out of your passion—instinctively you join it?*

RUSSELL: *I love those conversations. Again, that's my life. That's really the root motivation I have for anything. So anytime that comes up, I'm just all over it. To me it takes great restraint. I think sometimes the Holy Spirit gives insight, discernment so you can recognize when it's the right time to say something. And when it's time to hold back and not say anything.*

During this 45-minute conversation, Russell articulated the missional developments of his life as a teacher. I couldn't help but notice how he used the word "connection" five to six times to aptly describe how the church is not a place or location, but as God's missionary people who are everywhere engaged in the mission of Jesus.

Chapter Five

THE SOUL'S DESTINATION: Missional Visioning

"There comes a time in our spiritual growth when nothing will satisfy but a real encounter with the indwelling Christ."
—Howard Baker

In the last chapter, we discussed living in the Kingdom of God. Let me emphasize some additional thoughts. The Kingdom vision of Jesus is a Christ-centered vision rather than an ethical vision that stands alone. Jesus' Kingdom is one that places Him at the center not simply social justice. The Kingdom of God is the central vision of Jesus and should be ours as well.

Scot McKnight says,

"The big difference one notices in entering into the early churches is this: kingdom language is largely dropped and ecclesia (church) language is picked up. There are all kinds of issues here, not the least of which is that as the church trotted into its first decade the community became convinced of its "sectarian" status rather than a ruling status and this accounts for some, not all, of its switching languages. Along with this is that it became increasingly effective in the Roman Empire and its status was less and less of a power. I don't buy that it gave up its vision for Kingdom, but its language did shift as it realized its status." [1]

The Kingdom has always been the larger, more encompassing vision that Jesus has for us. We can experience this encompassing vision becoming central to us as well throughout the movements of our faith.

Revelation 21: 3 RSV tells us, *"Behold, the dwelling of God is with men. He will dwell with them, and they shall be his people..."*

Our inner world (heart and soul) becomes the dwelling of Jesus by His initiative and our response. This is where the vision of Jesus provides the soul's visioning reality needed for the missional path and the journey ahead.

"...and I shall dwell in the house of the Lord forever." Amen Psalm 23

The Psalmist did not suggest he would dwell in the actual Temple but his desire was to dwell forever in the presence of God. Just as it did for the Psalmist, Psalm 23 provides a simple way to express our own experience and to help us understand the movements of our faith.

As a result, this interior world becomes like the inner self of Jesus and the natural source of words and deeds that are characteristic of him as those set forth in Ephesians 2:19-22 RSV below:

"So then you are no longer strangers and sojourners, but you are fellow citizens with the saints and members of the household of God, built upon the foundation of the apostles and prophets, Christ Jesus himself being the cornerstone, in whom the whole structure is joined together and grows into a holy temple in the Lord; in whom you also are built into it for a dwelling place of God in the Spirit."

By the Spirit's enabling, dwelling presence we come to "have this mind among yourselves, which is your in Christ Jesus..." Philippians 2:5 RSV

Using the approach to the most of the psalms by Walter Brueggeman in his book *Praying the Psalms* and the progressions of Orientation (being securely oriented), Disorientation (being painfully disoriented), and Reorientation (being surprisingly reoriented). [1] Tracing the Psalmist's spiritual journey using Brueggemann's three-stage model of increasing appropriation of Christ by faith.

Brueggemann viewed the Psalms as seasons. Seasons of stability, seasons of upheaval and seasons of Joy. As we will see, Psalms 23 moves through all three.

The Psalms teach us how to pray when we do not have a clue what to say. The Psalms are utterly realistic in their portrayal of raw, human emotion before God. They help us face, recognize, and articulate the feelings that may be swirling undeciphered in our hearts. It brings about missional integrity with ourselves before God. So often we cover up our true feelings. We put on a happy face before God and we think if we pretend to be grateful or go through the motions of prayer, that somehow God will notice.

We can bring our entire lives before God. Sometimes we do not bring parts of our lives to God because we are ashamed about them. They may not make sense to us. But when we hide our hearts from God, we hide from the only one who can bring true healing and transformation. Dallas Willard says, "We can only hide from God if God hides from us. He gives us the privilege to hide."

The Dwelling Principle

In simple terms, this is the presence of Christ through the Holy Spirit. I use the metaphor of a "dwelling" or house to describe what I call "The Dwelling Principle."

Psalms 23 illustrates Bruggemanns' orientation, disorientation and reorientation. I have used the metaphor of a house to describe a similar path to follow as most of us would move about in our homes. They are:

- The Kitchen of the Soul
- The Basement of the Heart
- The Living Room of Human and Divine Presence

Imagine walking through these rooms in your own home. Now consider each room as a period of time, a decade, or a chapter in your life where you could identify the movements of your faith.

As you reflect on these concepts, it is important for you to remember that your faith can move through all of these rooms in one day or in a matter of hours. The key is being aware that Christ is dwelling with you even in those rooms where unpleasantness happens.

You will be able to trace your own spiritual journey using the "rooms" in a home metaphor which conceptualizes God as the one who has guided us. God leads us into the well-being of faith, helps us deal with faith when we doubt, and provides soul dwelling.

As you become more familiar with the Dwelling Principle, hopefully, you will come to see the advantage(s) and not the disadvantages of being where you are. Resist the temptation of to forcibly push your faith or the faith of others to a more comfortable environment. In each room, our faith experiences a new and unique divine layer of Christ's presence that you will not want to miss.

Kitchen of the Soul [Psalms 23:1-3]

The first three verses establish the experience or point of contact where the orientation describes our being cared for by God. It is the place where all our expectations of being a child of God are met. The downside is that we consume. It is the place where we love to hangout. It is here that we become genuinely good at living. The characteristics are hard to put into words exactly. We experience satisfaction, security, stability, adaptation, comfort, contentment well-being and consumption.

The conscious reality is that God is presiding, but not bothering. The unconscious reality comes to us in a question. Is this where I want to stay permanently, temporarily, or move through?

The Basement of the Heart [Psalms 23:4-5]

I am quite sure you have noticed the difference in language when the Psalmist begins to talk about walking through the valley. Notice how the Psalmist moves from discussing how Christ the Good Shepherd leads him to the right paths to walking through the valleys where evil and death are present. Yet, he discovers the presence of God there.

The characteristics of this place are danger, doubt, perplexity, fear, depression, evil, darkness, and presumption. It is a place spiritually where you feel that you have fallen off the side of a mountain.

Now imagine moving from the Kitchen of the Soul where all of your needs were met by the Almighty to the Basement of the Heart. This is the place where your heart does indeed drop.

Most of the basements that I know about are storage areas where one might find unopened boxes of possessions that do not deserve a public place. Sometimes those boxes represent portions of our lives that we no longer need or desire but do not have the courage to throw away.

Nevertheless, we see them again they can be subtle reminders of our former lives and we can become tempted by that life once more. The conscious reality can be alarming. It is so easy to lose faith when we are warmed by the furnace of doubt.

Once when I talked about this in a sermon in a church where I was serving as the associate pastor I invited responses from the congregation afterwards. One lady who had experienced the death of her husband who took his own life. With a trembling voice and tears, she said, "This is exactly where I am…in the basement of my heart. I would love to move to the kitchen where I could feel good about myself and my family." I responded, "Thank you for seeing your current reality. That is positive for you. Just remember that God presence is with you in the basement and when He has prepared you well enough, you'll move to the kitchen again."

This was a beautiful exchange of someone who was able to simply identify the movements of her faith. The unconscious reality for her and perhaps you as well is another question. "What have you learned about yourself in your own basement experiences of life?"

The Living Room of Human and Divine Presence [Psalms 23:6]

The language of the theologian Martin Buber aptly describes this as the "I-Thou Relationship." The conscious reality is the observation of where the dining host's presence resides. The characteristics of this room include worship, joy, rekindled faith, habitation, deeper trust, awareness, contemplative and dwelling.

Spiritually speaking this is the place where we commune and collaborate with God. This is what Richard Foster calls, "The With-God Life." Together with God, we dwell with God and He dwells with us. Or God abides with us and we abide in Him.

Applying the Dwelling Principle

We have a part to play in our spiritual transformation in that it requires our attentiveness and effort. We retreat to spend time alone with God. We identify the room where our faith now resides. We let the Scriptures shape us. We practice the presence of God. All of these things cultivate intimacy with God.

Before you go on to the next chapter, take a few minutes for the following exercise:

By reflecting upon your entire lifetime, can you identify the movements (rooms) where your faith resided during a crisis? During a time of celebration? During a time of closeness to God?

Chapter Six

THE SOUL'S SEARCHING: Missional Learning

"Many people think that what's written in the Bible has mostly to do with getting people into heaven—getting right with God, saving their eternal souls. It does have to do with that, of course, but not mostly. It is equally concerned with living on this earth—living well, living in a robust sanity."

—Eugene Peterson, The Message

Step Five, Missional Learning, is the central step in this book. In this step, we explore a learning revolution of training people to become missionaries to this culture and community and the bonus of finding freedom in real mission.

Much of this step is about the new reality of missional-driven leadership needed in the church today. A leadership laced with mission for people who are spiritually questing in the streets and looking for the church to come to them.

When our country was more industrialized and the nuclear family was the norm, the church was at the center of society. Today, things are much different, as you well know. The church can be the center of an individual's life, but the church is no longer the center of our culture. The church desperately needs to go to the streets.

Church laity can learn and want to be missionaries to their friends, neighbors, work associates, golfing partners, etc. In fact, they cannot understand why the church does not change course, find the missional path themselves, or ask some non-church people where the mission really is. They know.

Moreover, I believe there is a small band of entrepreneurs in every church who are often misunderstand, labeled, and marginalized who would love to have the church's blessing to be missional instead of giving their leftover time and energies after work and family to do church stuff.

Before we get into the elements of missional-driven leadership, I would like to tell this humorous story. A story that will serve well those of us who want to expand the Kingdom but not in opposition to, or in resistance to the church. We just want to be released to **be** the church.

A group of frogs was hopping contentedly through the woods when two of the frogs fell into a deep pit. The other frogs made a quick assessment of the situation and concluded that it was hopeless. They recommended that the frogs in the pit accept their fate and prepare to die. Sorrowfully they shouted down to the pit-confined frogs such encouraging words as: "save your energy," "give up," and "you're as good as dead."

One of the frogs bought into their perspective of the situation, gave up and died. While the other frog, who was deaf, thought the others were cheering him on. He continued to jump until he finally leapt so high that he jumped right out of his pit.

Having the right perspective is crucial for the North American church. The reality is that an insatiable desire for the church to drop all the "church stuff" really does exist. The appetite to "be the church" is represented by many who are disillusioned with the institution and many who are spiritually questing in places other than the church.

I don't know about you but today's hunger for spirituality has my attention. I hope it has your as well. For this reason, I am motivated to place myself at the center of a new missional reformation for the church that has lost its mission.

Before we get into this in detail, I want you to use your imagination. Imagine you are at mission control at NASA's space center and you are sitting at a control station where another space shuttle mission has reached the countdown sequence mode. All systems are set for launch.

Before the actual launch, the supporting structures, equipment, and crews stationed around the shuttle itself must back away before the engines start. Once the shuttle is launched and away, the control center continues to monitor and track the ship's trajectory and flight path. You must make sure in your monitoring that all the huge silos of fuel attached to the outer shell of the shuttle reach their burn point and breakaway into deep space so the shuttle itself has the freedom to navigate and pursue it prescribed space path.

Figure 6, on the following page, illustrates a Missional-Driven Leadership Model that can be utilized by traditional churches who desire to implement missional learning. I would suggest that a vote to do this would not work. Instead, the pastor and key leaders should decide to slowly energize but not timidly work with a handful of spiritually mature Christians who already see themselves as missionaries or at the very least have been exposed to some of the concepts put forth in this book. That way, they and the church can view the incremental progress of a few good men and women who "find the missional path."

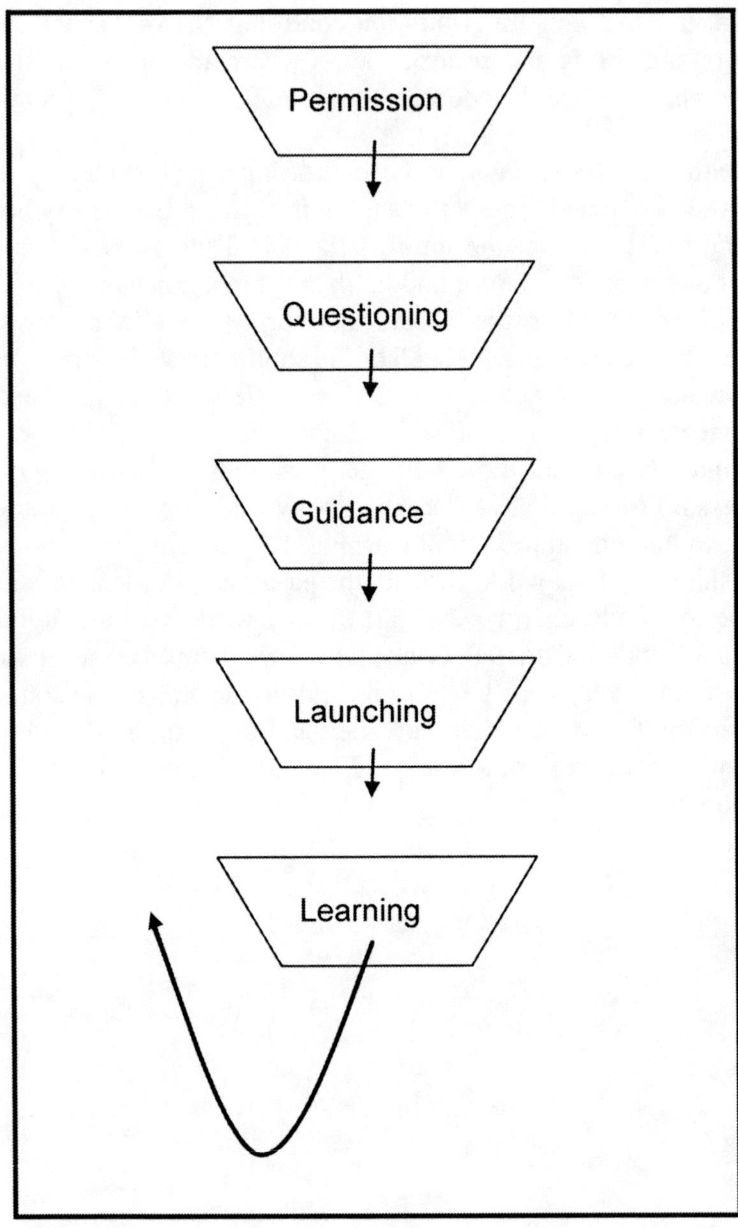

The elements of the model are Permission, Questioning, Guidance, Launching and Learning. It is absolutely critical that each element be thoroughly understood and completed before moving on to the next element. After the Learning element, the process is diagramed to be an on-going movement of the few good men and women who have been released to be missional.

At the end of the chapter, scriptural support for the model is provided. Although other accounts could be useful, Luke Chapter 9, at least for me, works well.

Permission

The element Permission is the release of an individual or church member from ministry to the body to being a missionary to the community. This is the blessing of the church to accomplish the Kingdom of God and to participate in God's redemptive purpose in the world.

In Luke 4:16-19 Jesus gave his inaugural sermon in his hometown synagogue and laid out his major themes. His mission targeted four groups: *the poor, the captives, the blind, and the oppressed.* He was a missionary to the mistreated, those who were not given justice, those who were abused, and those who found no recourse. Jesus promised *good news, release, sight, and freedom.* He claimed Isaiah 61 was about Himself and perhaps the Jubilee expectations of Leviticus 25. Then, the inauguration of the Kingdom was underway as He met people on the missional path.

Jesus was a complete frustration to political and church leaders who were out to earn votes, because his motivations were not controlled by self-interest. He cared passionately about those whom we would classify today as being completely "off the radar screen." He reached out to the poor, the very young and the very old, the mistreated and more.

Jesus had his authority, permission, and blessing in his Trinitarian relationship with the Father and the Holy Spirit. He fulfilled the work God had done and the scripture of the Old Testament is completed in his public ministry, his death and resurrection, his sending of the disciples and the sending of the Holy Spirit. He did what scripture had attempted to do for God's people and for the good of others in the world.

The Blessing of the Church

I cannot stress too much just how important the blessing of the church is in this leadership model. All the others elements are contingent on the leadership getting this one right. You do not want to run contrary to the church. As we pointed out earlier in the chapter, Jesus preached his inaugural mission sermon in his hometown and in the synagogue. The Apostle Paul did the same thing.

Paying close attention to the details of gaining the Permission or the blessing of the church yields identity just like calling our brother and sisters the children of God. In 1 John 3: 1, notice how the act of naming was significant. *"See what love the Father has given us, that we should be called children of God; and so we are."*

Why is a small activity such as paying attention to the significance of naming other brothers and sisters so huge? Because naming appropriately gives confidence to people. We all tend to live in a way that is consistent with our self-concept. No one can live or behave in a way that contradicts their sense of identity.

When the church releases a few people of its flock to be missionaries, they must be careful not to put these people in the position of feeling like or appearing to be a "renegade" in the face of others in the church who are doing ministry to the body. Those who minister and those who are missional both have a place in the church. Do you agree?

The evil one hammers away at us to keep us from seeing our true identity. Satan wants you to think you are unacceptable to God. So, one does not need to "get off on the wrong foot" with the church when all you want is for the church to release and affirm your missional work in the Kingdom.

The New Testament is filled with phrases and terms to re-orient your sense of identity. For instance:

"You are the light of the world."
"You are the salt of the earth."
"You are my friends."
"You are a joint-heir with Christ

"You are a part of the chosen race, a royal priesthood."
"You are a city set on a hill that cannot be hid."

Questioning

Once permission and in particular blessing has been granted by the church for those men and women who earnestly desire to see themselves as missionaries to their community, the essence of the missional activity must be weighed against the relevancy to the Kingdom and Christ's mission and redemptive purposes in the world.

If there is not a period of questioning and comfortability with the mission is not attained, then there is a strong possibility that the message will be compromised. Watch out for making a rock concert, a circus, a raffle and other things to build interest and attract people. These activities must not dishonor your identity.

There should be a significant amount of prayer and contemplation given to the subject. This is not about whether it is right or wrong to do it. It's much bigger than that (If it were only that simple).

Here are some questions to ask. Is this going to bring glory to God? Can the people who are involved and the onlookers view it with respect? Do they view it as respectable? Do you want your church to be known for this? Use the scripture as a baseline.

If we are unwilling to subject missional ambitions to the relevancy of Christ's message and Kingdom, we must be cautious because if we want it bad enough, we become spiritual contortionists—doing what is right in our own eyes. Would you rather go out on a missional adventure feeling 100% confident that you are doing this in the name of the Lord? Or, would you rather go feeling 70% confidence? You have to do it with no fear. If there is fear, then maybe you don't need to do it.

"So have no fear of them; for nothing is covered that will not be revealed, or hidden that will not be known." Matthew 10:26 RSV

Guidance

Permission granted by the church and questioning for relevance to the Kingdom are followed by Guidance. This part of the process is where we identify the people who are spiritually questing, but are not looking to with the church in their searching. Jesus hung out among the poor and the oppressed. He promised good news, release, sight and freedom. It was a reversal of the way things were for these groups. Things definitely changed for those who were willing to walk with Jesus. He recognized the systemic sin of Israel that manifested itself in the abuse of power and the abuse of the poor. Sin is never just personal, although it is that too. When we sin, we are affected, but also others around us, in our community, and in our society are affected. Sin is rebellion against God manifested in four directions: against God, self, others and the world. This means we cannot solve the sin problem in one direction with God. We must solve the problem through repentance and forgiveness in all four directions.[1]

This is much different than targeting a group with similar interest, talents, and activities as the ones you possess. Instead, more often than not, this Guidance challenges you to engage people whom you despise because of their language, their habits, and their behavior and they simply just do not look like you or agree with your taste.

For example, could you be a missionary to a homosexual who was spiritually questing for truth? Would you meet with him or her in public to discuss spirituality and Christ over coffee or a coke? Or, if a homosexual showed up at your church on Sunday for worship how would they be treated? Would you expect them to conform and confess their sin openly or would you rather they field the church's hints of rejection and hope that they not return?

When the country was reeling from Dan Brown's book about "The Da Vinci Code," many Christians decided that anyone who read the book was demon possessed and beyond the hope of the church until some ambitious denominational leaders saw it as an attention-grabbing marketing tool for the church. I know of several pastors who preached sermons about the Da Vinci Code but never read the book or talked with people who did. Can you imagine that? It appeared to me the church was only interested if they could somehow benefit from it through slick marketing purposes.

Underlying the popularity of The Da Vinci Code is the hunger and thirst of millions of Americans looking for spirituality. This is true for school shootings as well. Did you notice the huge VT letters enshrined with flowers, letters, and caring notes from praying students grieving after the killing of 32 students on the campus of Virginia Tech University earlier this year? It became a holy place where students, families, and faculty members could share their stories and value community.

Then are those groups of people who have what I call generic inspiration. They are regularly influenced by the genre of music and experience they listen to and the social issues of immigration justice for Hispanics, native-American people, the urban homeless and the Appalachian poor. They may not fly under a particular denomination or church but they are spiritually questing just the same.

As the world continues to flatten, we have the choice of expanding with it or getting squashed beneath it. Everything is global now. People think globally. And it should not surprise you that people are eager to find instant collaboration between the farthest corners of religion and spiritual talk. We are experiencing an unparalleled interconnectedness for transcendence and Christianity is not the only option available. When I first read Friedman's book, *The World is Flat*, I asked, "How technology and globalization would translate to the church's understanding of its own mission?"

Launching

You guessed it. This element is the "lift off." Finding the missional path is a "better late than never" for the church. When Jesus sent the disciples out, they went. If you are a pastor, let your people go. Allow them to see their home, their workplace, the neighborhood as their mission.

When they come back from the journey be there for them. Provide the necessary support and encouragement they need. It is paradoxical. Do not be afraid to lose these missionary individuals from being busy with church activity because the Kingdom will gain more. The people who want to find the missional path cannot be fruitful when they think they are being held captive by all the church stuff. Keep in mind we are not talking about everyone in your church.

Learning

Giving up control is pertinent to missional-driven leadership. However, giving up support and learning is not optional. The account of Luke gives us a snapshot of Jesus being "on time" for the return of the disciples.

"On their return the apostles told him what they had done. And he took them and withdrew apart to a city called Bethsaida. When the crowds learned it, they followed him; and he welcomed them and spoke to them of the kingdom of God and cured those who had need of healing.

Now the day began to wear away; and the twelve came and said to him, 'Send the crowd away to go into the villages and country round about, to lodge and get provisions; for we are here in a lonely place. But he said to them, 'You give them something to eat.' They said, 'We have no more than five loaves and two fish—unless we are to go and buy food for all these people.' For there were about five thousand men. And he said to his disciples, 'make them sit down in companies, about fifty each. And they did so, and made them all sit down. And taking the five loaves and the two fish he looked up to heaven, and blessed and broke them, and gave them to the disciples to set before the crowd. And all ate and were satisfied. And they took up what was left over, twelve baskets of broken pieces.

Now it happened that as he was praying alone the disciples were with him; and he asked them, "Who do the people say that I am?" Luke 9:10-18 RSV

Several interesting things are going on in this passage.

1. When the disciples returned, they to Jesus what they had done.
2. Jesus took them to Bethsaida for learning time.
3. The crowds followed Jesus and the disciples
4. Jesus modeled a sense of urgency to be missional even when the disciples needed his attention
5. At the end of the day, the disciples wanted to send the crowds away.

6. Jesus performed the miracle of the loaves and fish to feed 5000 people.
7. Jesus prayed with the disciples and ask questions to find out what they had heard about him while they were doing mission.
8. Eight days later Jesus took James, John and Peter to the mountain to pray.

The element of Learning is a place of renewal, retooling, and learning from each other through their stories about their missional experiences. This is exactly the kind of venue missionaries need before they go out again.

Notice Figure 6 again in this chapter. The line connecting each element continues through the Learning element and the entire process begins again. Keep in mind that those who have been through the process need the continuation of the process because they are finding freedom in real mission and the process strengthens the connection of everyone including the church.

Chapter Seven

THE SOUL'S SERIOUSNESS: Missional Accountability

"Turning members into ministers hasn't worked for another reason. Church members don't want to do what they see many ministers doing. On the one hand, when they see ministers being where the action is, helping people, turning lives around, partnering with God's work in the world, they line up. On the other hand, too many church members view clergy as professional ministers who have been cranked out by the church industry to manage church stuff. They have not been exposed to church leaders who are leaders of a movement"

–Reggie McNeal[1]

Finding the missonal path is incarnational because it is a purely decentralized path. The path leads to an incarnational community and goes into cultures that already exist in order to reach them with the Gospel. The explorers on the path believe that God is already working in these cultures and therefore, their role as missionaries is not to bring God into **their** group or take that out of its culture into a sacred space. Instead, they help others to see how God is already working in and around them in the ordinary as well as the miraculous.

Greater numbers of people are providing leadership today because they are leading from unusual places. They often lack resources and formal training, but are willing to risk responding to the missional call of God. They often lack the established structures and a well-funded organization, but they have the approval of God.

A few Christian people are being missional and are unaware of it when they engage culture in malls, internet café's, bookstores, coffee shops, etc. For the most part the North American church is not. Churches all over the country are distracted and many have left their *first* love. This is the case I have made in the book.

I believe many church members, not all of them, want to live missional lives and not be captured by the same "church stuff" that occupies paid professionals. For too long now, the church has believed the best way to grow people is to get them involved in church ministry activity. The problem now is the idea that God has gifted people only for church jobs and that is missionally counter-productive. Many of the people in our churches today do not want to do what we ministers do. Instead, they want to be missionaries where their greatest connection and greatest influence lies.

Inevitably, there will be ministry activity in every church that you cannot stop doing. I am not advocating doing away with your ministries and programs nor the people who serve in those capacities. I am only suggesting that some people do not fit the "every member a minister" role. Some have done very well at this and will continue to do what they are doing. Others, may need to be reassigned or redeployed depending upon their giftedness and the churches resources.

As I stated earlier in the book, I am suggesting that pastors and leaders intentionally release a few good men and women to become missionaries in their own zip code. Shifting your perspective away from ministry to **include being missional** will not be easy. Change never happens overnight. Change is painful.

As a leader you may ask, "How can I hold myself accountable to make sure I am developing a missional perspective and not just putting a new twist on ministry?"

That is a very good question. Hopefully, this chapter will offer some "hand holds" useful to you.

The hard thing is that, as pastors, though we find ourselves saying these words, we are frequently frustrated when our people do not step up and do it. But do not blame your people. They want to contribute, to be missional, and to do Kingdom work. They do want to step up. But faced with a world that is so ambivalent about their church involvement—recognized when the job is done, dismissive when it doesn't—they just do not know how.

This book will help them. It will be refreshing and instill in them a lifelong way to impact lives and feel good about it without beating themselves up, even if the people they have been missionaries to, never come to the church. Why? They have been introduced to the vision of God for their lives and that is what is important anyway.

Consequently, you cannot transform your church members, your ministry team, your colleagues, or your entire congregation until you know how to transform your own missional life. As the airlines would say, you need to put on your own oxygen mask before you start trying to help those around you. Only then, teach others what you have learned and experienced.

Navigate the Missional Terrain Yourself

First of all, you cannot teach what you do not know. Pastors, go before your leaders or church board and ask for permission to be missional one or two days out of every week. Then push yourself out of your comfort zone. Build friendships and surface level relationships with people who are noticeably different from you. Then listen. There is nothing stopping you at this point. The only thing that stops you is any preconceived entrenched beliefs you may have.

Think about it. Most of us pastors live insulated lives. We are surrounded with Christian people. We visit them, call them, and meet with them. Do you have any friends outside of your church? Do you have any friends that you see on a weekly basis who are worldly? I hope so. You need them and they certainly need you. So go ahead and be the first to navigate the missional terrain. Find the missional path and point others to it.

Pastors, in one of your board meetings, suggest that each member do something missional the next week. Give some ideas to chew on. Tell them it is OK with you for them to show up in some unexpected places and unfamiliar territory while engaging others. Discuss with them the Missional-Driven Leadership Model and drive home the importance of permission and the blessing of the church.

Figure 7 is a Missional Checklist you and others can use to hold yourself accountable to being missional. This would be a useful tool to use after three to six months into a new relationship. They will appreciate you giving them the opportunity to give honest feedback.

I am sure there are better ways to make ourselves missionally accountability. Perhaps you can develop your own practical tools for measuring how well you are doing. Should you come up with anything, feel free to contact me.

Figure 7, Missional Checklist

Missional Checklist

Instructions: Circle the X that best indicates how you felt during your interaction with _________ (first name only)

Greeted you and told you their name. Interested in you as a person.	←X—X—X—X—X→	Said they represented a certain church. Just wanted me to come to church.
Talked most about Jesus.	←X—X—X—X—X→	Talked mostly about the church.
Talk about God's vision for my life.	←X—X—X—X—X→	Tried to make me feel guilty.
Talked about their love of God and people.	←X—X—X—X—X→	Talked about what the church has to offer.

It Takes Only One Who Finds the Missional Path

People, like yourself, who find the missional path have the opportunity and the ability to bring other people onto the path. Why? Because like me, you are making lasting change little by little and you are satisfied with that. And so am I.

Where once, leadership was seen to come from the front, from appointed person in defined roles, from paid professionals, and from the few to the many; now leadership often comes from the one walking beside us. Instead of the Wizard, it is Dorothy who has wisdom. Instead of Aragon or Gandalf, it is the Frodo's of this world with their obedience who will be the fulcrum for change.

Remember your first love.

Jesus said,

"Go therefore and make disciples of all nations, baptizing them in the name of the Father and of the Son and of the Holy Spirit, teaching them to observe all that I have commanded you; and lo, I am with you always, to the close of the age." Matthew 28:19-20 RSV

Chapter Eight

20 Missional Ideas

This is certainly not an exhaustive list. Keep an open mind with these ideas. Try not to discount the entire list if a few of them do not fit with you. However, try a few and push yourself out of your comfort zone. Be considerate, sensitive and aware of cultural and other differences. Most of all do not let fear stand in your way.

1. Instead of recommending someone find a church to attend and get their life straight, encourage them to listen to the voice of God and try to discern what He is say to them. Encourage them to do this for two weeks, then look for a church to attend.
2. Spend time every week with people who do not attend church.
3. If someone asks you "Where's your church?" take the opportunity to help them view the church as people instead of a place. Then, later in the conversation, you can give them the name of the church and the location.
4. The words missional is a descriptive term If someone asks for a definition, tell them it describes being a missionary in your zip code, your favorite hangout, your workplace, etc. Then, be Jesus to them.
5. When your work colleagues meet after work at a home or restaurant, go with them even though alcoholic beverages

may be served. Be salt and light to them by showing you are not ashamed to have fun with them.

6. Hopefully a significant number of your friends are unbelievers. Jesus seemed to spend a lot of time with unbelievers in the gospels and they were apparently comfortable with Him for the most part. It was the religious hypocrites who were threatened and could not stand Him.
7. At the end of each day, write down two things that went right for you, but after reflecting on them, you realize they seemed to be a God moment. Getting in the habit of looking at those God moments around you at the office, home, or attending your son's baseball game will be spiritually rewarding.
8. Invite people in your neighborhood to your house for a meal or barbecue. It will give you a chance to meet their families and will let them meet your family. Avoid bringing up the subject of church. If a spiritual conversation arises, let it come to you. Inviting someone into your home is a big step and it builds friendship and opportunities for open communication.
9. Each day, spend five minutes looking for someone who needs your encouragement. When you spot them, engage with positive conversation and friendliness.
10. Make a list of what you know about each person you work with and each person that you give leadership to. What do they do at work? Do they have kids? If so, what are their names, and how old are they? Ask yourself: Which employee do I know the least about? Take time today to visit that person to get to know them better.
11. Each time you fill your gas tank, make it a point that same day to fuel your friends with appreciation and thanks.
12. Learn to be an active listener. Practice eye contact. Ask follow-up questions. The more you demonstrate you can be trusted with concerns and ideas, the more people will open up to you.
13. Extend yourself on a personal level. The next time one of your friends reaches a milestone, invite the person to a restaurant.

14. Study the Kingdom passages in the Bible and spend contemplative prayer about the redemptive purpose of God in this world.
15. Thinking missionally is a new way of thinking. Like anything else that is new, change will not come easily. What is required is a real passion, a Kingdom vision, and a whole lot of courage.
16. Part of being missional is engaging people in their language and on their turf. Avoid making people feel guilty over their sin before you have shared God's vision for their life. Remember, we are to share GOOD NEWS!
17. Practice listening to spiritual conversations with your sincere interest focused on the individual not their beliefs and opinions.
18. Go to a nearby park and sit on a bench with strangers. Engage or join conversation with them.
19. Visit a nearby Barnes & Noble bookstore or internet café and just listen for spiritual conversations. You may be surprised.
20. Pray for one opportunity each week and tell your spouse or your pastor about it so they will hold you accountable. Ask them to ask you what you did with your opportunity. Read the parable of the talents.

Endnotes

Introduction

1. Guinness, Os. (1984). *The Gravedigger File: Papers on the Subversion of the Modern Church.* Downers Grove, Illinois: InterVarsity Press. pp. 43-44, emphasis added

Chapter 1

1. Casey, Michael. (1996). *Toward God: The Ancient Wisdom of Western Prayer.* Triumph Books. p. 5.

2. Kerkegaard, Soren. (1951). *Either/Or*, w Vols., Trans. Walter Lowrie. University Press: Princeton, NJ.

3. Mair, George. (2005). *A Life With Purpose*. New York, New York: Berkley Books. p. 114.

4. Barna, George. (2005). *One in Three Adults is Unchurched..* The Barna Update. March 28 Internet Article. http://www.barna.org. p. 1.

5. Barna, George. (2005). *One in Three Adults is Unchurched..* The Barna Update. March 28 Internet Article. http://www.barna.org. p. 1-2.

6. Mair, George. (2005). *A Life With Purpose*. New York, New York: Berkley Books. p. 130.

7. McManus, Erwin Raphael. (2005). *The Barbarian Way*. Nelson Books: Nashville, Tennessee. p. 17.

8. Burke, John. (2005). *No Perfect People Allowed*. Grand Rapids, Michigan: Zondervan. p. 100.

9. McManus, Erwin Raphael. (2005). *The Barbarian Way*. Nelson Books: Nashville, Tennessee. p. 13.

10. Peterson, Eugene H. (2005). *Christ Plays in Ten Thousand Places*. William B. Eerdmans Publishing Company: Grand Rapids, Michigan. p. 261.

11. Rainer, Thom S. Discipleship and the Church Growth Movement. Internet Article. http://www.churchcentral.com May 17, 2005.

12. Peterson, Eugene H. (2005). *Christ Plays in Ten Thousand Places*. William B. Eerdmans Publishing Company: Grand Rapids, Michigan. p. 261.

13. McNeal, Reggie. (2003). The Present Future. San Francisco, California: 13. Jossey-Bass. P. 32. 14.

14. Gibbs, Eddie. (2000). *Church Next: Quantum Changes in How We Do Ministry*. Downers Grove, Illinois: InterVarsity Press. p. 27.

15. Zahariades, Jason. (2005). *Detoxing from Church*. BloggerNet. Internet Article. http://www.theofframp.org pp. 1-3.

16. Ibid., p. 3.

17. Siddall, Ann. (2004). *The Spirituality Revolution and the Invitations for the Church.* Adelaide West Uniting Church Spirituality Centre. Internet Source. p. 6.

18. Guinness, Os. (1984). *The Gravedigger File: Papers on the Subversion of the Modern Church.* Downers Grove, Illinois: InterVarsity Press. P. 3,

19. Mair, George. (2005). *A Life With Purpose.* New York, New York: Berkley Books. pp. 91.

20. Mair, George. (2005). *A Life With Purpose.* New York, New York: Berkley Books. pp. 92-93.

21. Barna, George. (2005). *One in Three Adults is Unchurched..* The Barna Update. March 28 Internet Article. http://www.barna.org. p. 91.

22. Guinness, Os. (1993). *Dining with the Devil.* Grand Rapids, Michigan: Baker Book House. pp. 20-21.

23. Rainer, Thom S. Discipleship and the Church Growth Movement. Internet Article. http://www.churchcentral.com May 17, 2005.

24. Guinness, Os. (1993). *Dining with the Devil.* Grand Rapids, Michigan. Baker Book House. p. 32.

25. Pearcy, Nancy. (2004). *Total Truth.* Wheaton, Illinois: Crossway Books. p. 44.

26. Guinness, Os. (1984). *The Gravedigger File: Papers on the Subversion of the Modern Church.* Downers Grove, Illinois: InterVarsity Press. pp. 43- 44, emphasis added

27. Whitman, Christine Todd. (2005). *It's My Party Too.* New York: The Penguin Press. p. 74.

28. Pearcy, Nancy. (2004). *Total Truth*. Wheaton, Illinois: Crossway Books. p. 44.

29. Ibid., p. 44

30. White, James Emery. (2004). *Serious times*. Downers Grove, Illinois. InterVarsity Press. pp. 137-138.

31. Wallis, Jim. (2005). *God's Politics*. New York, New York: Harper SanFranscisco. p. 68.

Chapter 2

1. Thomas, Scott. (2004). *Twelve Marks of a Missional Church*. Internet Article found on website http://www.acts29network.org.

2. Goheen, Michale W. *Notes Toward a Frmework for a Missional Hermeneutic*. Article on The Gospel and Our Culture Network www.gocn.org. December 11, 2006

Chapter 3

1. Dietrich Bonhoeffer, *Life Together* (from ch.5, "Confession and Communion"
2. Menken, Alan and Stephen Schwartz, song *"God Help the Outcasts"* taken from the soundtrack to The Hunchback of Notre Dame.

3. Hall, Chad, "Missional Possible: Steps to Transform A Consumer Church Into A Missional Church." Leadership Magazine. Winter 2007 Issue. P. 35.

Chapter 4

1. Peterson, Eugene H. (2005). *Christ Plays in Ten Thousand Places*. William B. Eerdmans Publishing Company: Grand Rapids, Michigan. p. 335.

2. Hunsberger, George. (1998). "Missional Vocation—Called and Sent to Represent the Reign of God" quotation from Missional Church, edited by Darrell Guder. Eerdmans: Grand Rapids, Michigan. P. 82

3. Peterson, Eugene H. (2005). *Christ Plays in Ten Thousand Places*. William B. Eerdmans Publishing Company: Grand Rapids, Michigan. p. 335.

Chapter 5

1. An internet blog post from Scot McKnight on "The Kingdom of God" at www.jesuscreed.blogspot.com

2. Brueggerman, Walter. (1982). *Praying the Psalms*. Saint Mary's Press: Winona, Minnesota. p. 43.

Chapter 6

1. An internet blog post from Scot McKnight on "Emerging Movement, Embracing Grace" at Missional in Seattle 3. www.jesuscreed.org

Chapter 7

1. McNeal, Reggie. (2003). *The Present Future*. San Francisco, California: Jossey-Bass. p. 46.

The Author

Barry E. Winders is a missional coach for Ministry Indicators of Jackson, Missouri. He has been in ministry for 36 years serving as pastor, staff member, and consultant.

His writings and seminars have impacted thousands of church leaders to local churches and various denominational groups.

Winders earned both his B.A. (1980) in Religious Studies and D.Min. (2001) in Leadership at Oakland City University in Indiana. He has also earned an A.A. and Th.M.

He is continuing further studies at the Saint Paul School of Theology in Kansas City, Missouri.

He is a United Methodist pastor and lives with his wife Carmen in Jackson, Missouri.

They have one daughter and two grandchildren.

Printed in the United States
90316LV00008B/201/A

9 781602 668171